DREAMING
YOUR REAL
SELF

DREAMING YOUR REAL SELF

A Personal Approach to Dream Interpretation

Joan Mazza, M.S.

A PERIGEE BOOK

A Perigee Book
Published by The Berkley Publishing Group
A division of Penguin Putnam Inc.
375 Hudson Street
New York, NY 10014

Copyright © 1998 by Joan Mazza, M.S.
Book design by Lisa Stokes
Cover design and photo collage by Wendy Bass
Cover photograph of woman's face © Telegraph/FPG

First edition: July 1998

Published simultaneously in Canada.

The Penguin Putnam Inc. World Wide Web site address is
http://www.penguinputnam.com

Library of Congress Cataloging-in-Publication Data

Mazza, Joan.
   Dreaming your real self : a personal approach to dream
interpretation / Joan Mazza.
       p.   cm.
   "A Perigee book."
   Includes bibliographical references and index.
   ISBN 0-399-52414-2
   1. Dreams.   2. Dream interpretation.   3. Symbolism (Psychology)
I. Title.
BF1078.M32 1998   97-40741
135'.3—dc21   CIP

Printed in the United States of America

10 9 8 7 6 5 4 3

This book is dedicated with love to Joyce Sweeney: admired author, writing mentor, idea sharer, relationship coach, best friend, true sister, and fellow dreamer

CONTENTS

ACKNOWLEDGMENTS

As in any exploration and educational journey, the many dreamworkers who have come before me provided the groundwork for my current path through their books, lectures, educational materials, and thoughtful insights. My thanks to all of them.

I would also like to express my gratitude to the many people who encouraged me and contributed in some way to the making of this book: John Dufresne, one of my writing teachers; Noreen Wald, whose expert assistance in the preparation of the proposal of this book helped immeasurably; Jimmy Barkan, my yoga teacher, who taught me about discipline, patience, and persistence; Dianne Grandstrom, who offered in-house wisdom, advice, and editing during the last stage of work on this book; and all my other friends at Twin Oaks Community, who encouraged me and brainstormed with me, even when my values were different from theirs. I especially thank Twin Oakers for being willing to have me offer my first public dream workshop at their Women's Gathering.

A heartfelt thank you to my nephew, Justin Coppolino, who

kept my printers and copier healthy and supplied me with replacement toner cartridges.

My appreciation, too, to my agent, Lori Perkins, who saw the value of this work and encouraged me from the start and who continues to keep me writing; and to my editor at Perigee Books, Sheila Curry, who made excellent suggestions on ways to improve this book in tone and clarity.

Words are inadequate for me to express how much I value the support of all my friends and professional associates who believed in me and encouraged me to keep writing: Linda Altman, Shirley and Ike Attias, Fred Bacher, Sandy Bandstra, Norma Berkman, Heidi Boehringer, Mary Beth Busutil, Linda Chapman, Carol Collins, Betty Dodson, James Goodman, Myra Gross, Virginia Heinlein, Jay Johnson, Rosemary Jones, Fern Knicos, Gail Knowland, Joan Lindsay, Marj Lyons, Stuart and Joan McIver, Richard Nathanson, Arnie Perlstein, John Reininger, Gale St. John, Candy Schloesser, Naomi Seijo, Mimi Shapiro, Edith Sloan, John Stafford, Marie Stewart, Dan Suchman, Rosemarie Uman, Archie Wilson, and my fellow members of The Book Group of South Florida who have sustained my sense of being a writer. My thanks particularly to the participants in my dream workshops who taught me so much and gave permission to use their dreams as examples.

My gratitude also goes out to Phil, who understood when I needed to work at times when we wanted to play, and who shared his space with me so I could have a writing retreat in the last phase of this book.

INTRODUCTION

THERE ARE MANY WAYS TO LOOK AT DREAMS, and many of them have value. This book presents a practical approach to dreamwork that emphasizes the usefulness of dream messages. We will see how a dream gives information that is useful at the time of the dream in the everyday issues of the dreamer's life. We will delve into the language and messages of dream meanings and how they can be retrieved and translated. We will explore how to understand the meaning of dreams with a wide variety of techniques. We will look at common dreams and their personal relevance. We will see how the messages of a dream can be taken into action and thus make positive life changes and improve relationships.

There are other books that explore the metaphysical meanings and the possibility of alternate universes, past and future lives and how these subjects manifest in dreams. *Dreaming Your Real Self* focuses on what a dream today can do for the dreamer now. It will emphasize the psychological and spiritual work that can be done by living with ourselves and those around us, just as they are, in exactly the circumstances we are in now.

Not surprisingly, if you bring a dream to several dreamworkers, you will get several possible interpretations from each one. More than a difference in the work or the correctness of certain techniques over others, this range of interpretation is evidence of the richness of dreams.

Some consider dreams to be the meaningless random firing of neurons in the brain while we sleep, but how do random firings explain the occurrence of recurrent dreams and themes? Would only certain neurons fire and give us the same pictures over and over again without their holding any special meaning for the dreamer?

While dreams do have meaning, we can never know what they mean in an objective Absolute Truth kind of way because things only have the meanings we give them. Even though pictures in our mind may only just be pictures, we, as humans who seek patterns and meanings, want to give value and purpose to them. So just as the story someone makes up from a picture in a psychological test tells us something about that person and the way he/she organizes images into personal meanings, dreams can provide similar revelations. Dreamwork is more about exploring and learning than it is about finding any True Meaning or Final Answer.

Some people approach dreamwork with the expectation of finding the correct meaning of a dream. They want an answer—a single, accurate answer—as if they were doing a math problem that has only one correct solution. Throughout this book, I will refer to layers of meanings rather than to any one meaning. When doing dreamwork, the dreamer will often have an *aha* moment, a recognition of what the dream is really about. It's important not to stop there, but to go on to discover more meanings, and more possible meanings, knowing they may all be right in different ways.

*   *   *

Dreaming has intrigued me all of my life. In adolescence, vivid and highly emotional dreams got my attention. My sexual dreams were at odds with my waking beliefs; they did not reflect what I had been taught good girls were supposed to think, feel, and act. Why was I dreaming these weird pictures and why did I do things in my dreams I would never do in waking life?

In my twenties, I entered psychotherapy with a psychiatrist. He, too, had an interest in dreams, and we spent much of my therapy on dreamwork. Starting with that experience, I began my own study, which continues today. My best education, however, has been and still is, working with the dreams of people who come to my dream groups and workshops and share themselves in this personal way.

You might find it helpful to come to dreamwork with a spirit of curiosity by asking: I wonder what this dream is telling me! It has been my experience that people are very smart in their dreams. With the insights they gain from dream exploration, they are able to become much more clear about themselves and their next steps. For me, dreams are puzzles to be solved or treasure maps to be deciphered. I delight in decoding these mysteries, but I also enjoy discovering many possible solutions, each of them offering information dreamers can put into action with their hearts and minds.

From this information, the dreamer opens a doorway to self-understanding and growth. I, too, walk through this doorway, ready to learn and make discoveries about myself as well as the dreamer. As a dreamworker, I sometimes open doors for others, and beckon them in. Some only want to look inside; others come for the dance. When we work in groups, we each look at the dream messages in terms of our own lives. We see that these messages can be a source of wisdom for more than just the dreamer. By sharing our dreams, each of us has several experiences of the magical *aha* of insight.

Many people wonder how their weird and frightening dreams

or their dream style could contain any wisdom at all. When I speak publicly, people often ask whether I have ever heard of a particular dream image or pattern of dreaming. The person might say, "I only remember my dreams when I take naps." Between the lines, the person is probably asking if this is a normal kind of dreaming. I respond, "If you dream this way, it's normal for you. For the dreamer, the dream is always normal. That's how you dream and how you remember your dreams."

While some people occasionally use dreams to diagnose patients and give them a label for their illness, I believe the dream is one of the best places to look for a person's mental health and wisdom. In dream images and actions, we will find the sensible view missing in waking life, often with a larger spiritual or global message cradling the specific dream message for the day. The richness of dreams is an opportunity for us to explore what it means to be human, to see how much alike we all are while at the same time expressing our universal qualities with charming individuality.

Dreams provide the clues to our essence and our mission or purpose for being. Our "symptoms" and "dysfunctional behaviors," as James Hillman reminds us in *The Soul's Code* (1996), are clues to who we truly are. Our dreams contain the metaphors of our lives, often pointing the way to right relationship, right livelihood, right attitude, speech, and action.

Through my work as a psychotherapist in private practice and as a seminar leader, my primary goal is to create a safe space for others to find out who they are and what they want, especially when it doesn't conform with the values and expectations of the culture and society in which they live. Whose ideas do you hold? What do you believe? Are these concepts yours or what you were taught you *should* believe?

Too many of us have been molded and shaped to conform to the wishes of our families, our religions, or the culture and society as a whole. We have discarded who we really are for a false self that has often left us empty and with a nagging sense of dissatisfaction. At midlife or later, we may realize we have spent most of our lives being what someone else wanted us to be.

Through dreamwork, you can reclaim your real self, including exploring the possibility of living outside conventional boundaries. Dreamwork can provide pivotal moments so that you might have a shift in your thinking that can lead you to find who and what you truly are.

I believe creativity and joy of living largely come from energy that is all too often suppressed by too many rules. This energy is often within our sexual self, which is inhibited by an antiquated and erroneous so-called morality that encourages miscommunication with ourselves and others. Through dreamwork, we can not only question authority, but we might also discover how our behavior is a rebellion against society's norms. Perhaps the dream is suggesting we should look at how these norms stifle our authenticity and creativity. I believe we must frequently question our most cherished beliefs with the anticipation of discovery.

Through dreamwork and through the choices that become available to you from dreams' interpretations, you will have an opportunity to capitalize on your own strengths to overcome weaknesses, to have a new way to see yourself and your world. Stephen Covey says, "Argue for your weakness and it's yours." Once we get past the bad feelings and the weird and scary images of the dream, there will be an *aha:* a moment of insight and delight. If we see our defects, we may not like what we see, but the vision also gives us the power to change what we don't like about ourselves. We can also tap into the hidden talents we know we have within us but may be unable to access during our daily lives of chores, work, and responsibilities.

On the Internet, we are encouraged to post our messages with the standard qualifiers: IMO (in my opinion), IME (in my experience), and YMMV (your mileage may vary). Please add these qualifiers to every sentence in this book.

If you understand things differently from the way I do, I say, "Hurray!" I want to lean forward and say, "Tell me how you see it. Isn't that interesting!"

one

Why Do Dreamwork?

THROUGHOUT HISTORY, PEOPLE HAVE BEEN fascinated by dreams and what they might mean. They have wondered where dreams come from, why we have them, and what message might be hidden in their tangled threads of images, feelings, and impossible events. There are ancient texts that give explanations of dreams. In the Christian tradition, as well as in other religions, God speaks through dreams or sends an angel into dreams with important messages.

At various times, dreams have been thought to be messages from God, guardian angels, the spirit world, the Higher Self, and the Shadow. They have been believed to be prophecies of the future, a statement of our truest nature, and expressions of our aggression, sexual desires, wishes, and fears. They are considered to be excursions into other worlds, journeys made when our soul leaves our bodies. Some say dreams are the voice of our soul or our spiritual nature.

In many ways, dreams are all of these and more. Each dream comes with a message. More accurately, it comes with several messages. Wherever we may believe the message originates, there is little doubt for people who have worked with their dreams that they offer us important and useful information.

With Freud's publication of *The Interpretation of Dreams* in 1900, the analysis of dreams began to be seen as a pathway to understanding the innermost workings of the mind. Freud believed that most dreams dealt with sex and aggression. Not surprisingly, that's what he found. Jung, in conflict with Freud, believed dreams served more functions than simply the discharge of instinctual energies associated with forbidden impulses. He believed dreams have a spiritual component and often show how the dreamer is becoming more whole, more in harmony with himself and others, as well as finding his place in the universe. If you do dreamwork with a Jungian therapist, you will find the Jungian themes in your dreams. If you work with a Freudian, you will find sex and aggression. As in much of life, you find what you are looking for and you get what you expect.

While both Freud and Jung opened the door to dreamwork at a level previously unheard of, modern dreamworkers have taken us further. While incorporating many of the earlier ideas, they have learned and taught how much more dreams have to offer.

Throughout this book, I will refer to modern dreamworkers and their different styles of working with dreams, including Fritz Perls, Ann Faraday, Jeremy Taylor, and Gayle Delaney.

WHERE DREAMS COME FROM

While we are all curious about where, exactly, dreams originate, so far, there is no way for us to know. Having a belief that dreams come from God, our deceased loved ones, or our Higher Selves, which may each be different ways of describing the same phenomenon, can help us to work with dreams because it gives us a structure or a model for understanding our dreams. However, rather than wonder about where dreams originate, I prefer to concentrate on their content and meaning. Having worked with dreams for many years, I feel confident that their source is both benevolent and wise, even when the dream presents the information in frightening and grotesque images. I know there is wisdom there that can help me and others to live more responsibly and joyfully if we listen to the messages of the dream, regardless of their possible source.

WHAT WE DREAM ABOUT

Dreams can be about anything and everything. They have as much variety and uniqueness of content as do the people who dream them. What each of us seems to dream about, however, are those issues that are of most concern to us. We dream about what is important in our lives at the time of the dream and we dream about our core issues: those concerns that permeate our lives, such as a desire for security or success, a need to be accepted or noticed, fears of abandonment or disaster. We dream about whatever is the focus of our attention in our waking life, especially in the hours just before the dream, which is one of the reasons why an individual's dream will have repeating patterns, images, and themes. The same pictures and melodies will come up again and again, telling the story we tell ourselves in different ways throughout our lives as we come to terms with who we are and our place in the world.

WHY WE DREAM

Dream researchers have discovered that if you wake a person during the sleep stage of rapid eye movement (REM), you are more likely to get a dream report. Dreaming occurs at other sleep stages, but most studies have been done during REM sleep because the rapid eye movements can be seen by the researcher in time to wake the dreamer while the dream is in progress.

Dream research also reveals that there appears to be a biological basis for dreaming. Nearly all mammals studied demonstrate that they dream—at least by a measurement of REM during sleep.

Dreamtime seems to be when we assimilate the day's events, incorporate information into our memory, and try to finish the emotional and psychological concerns we were left with when we went to sleep. Those things we thought we let go of—the slight, the insult, the sense of incompetence or embarrassment—these come back in our dreams so that we can redo or undo or understand what happened. Through dreaming, we try to achieve closure on what we didn't finish that day.

Let us suppose I say hello to someone at work and don't receive an answer. The person looks up with a dazed expression and then looks away. If, on some level I feel hurt or confused, I am likely to have a dream to better deal with that event. The dream might offer a possible solution to a problem or it might give, by comparing it to an old event, an explanation for why I experienced uncomfortable emotions. I might dream about childhood friends who didn't want to play with me or didn't invite me to a party. The action of the dream may point out a way to make sense of my reaction to why my co-worker didn't respond when I said hello today.

Intellectually, I know she was probably busy, preoccupied, or didn't hear me, and that's what I told myself while my rational mind was operating. At a deeper level, her lack of response might have hurt me. This discomfort brings up familiar feelings of rejection. My unconscious compares it with old events and tries to make sense of it based on my experience. The dream brings to the surface the deeper feelings that I denied in my conscious, waking, practical life. The dream tries to tie up the loose ends of the previous day.

Similarly, if I am angry with someone during the day but didn't express it or recognize it, then I'm likely to express these feelings more fully in a dream. I might tell someone off, call him or her names, or run away from someone who is out to get me—

all possible expressions of my own anger that I didn't acknowledge in waking life.

We all bury our emotions for one reason or another. Often we do it by telling ourselves our feelings aren't reasonable or appropriate to the situation. This will be particularly true when we have feelings that are unacceptable to us. Feelings that seem too powerful might be anger, sexual or sensual desire, or our needs for intimacy and closeness. These emotions may call up the messages we received as children that it's not okay to have these thoughts and reactions. If we were discouraged from being generous and helpful to others, we might not be able to consciously act on these positive impulses. Any impulse we have been taught to reject may make us afraid of our vulnerability or our power to harm others. The dream offers us an opportunity to complete and/or to integrate these emotions.

Sometimes in our dreams, we anticipate future events, preparing ourselves in our sleep. Many of us have had the experience of going to bed before an important interview or special occasion and dreaming about sleeping too late, not being able to find our shoes, arriving unprepared, forgetting important papers, or going in our pajamas. Perhaps our unconscious is warning us of all the things that could go wrong. We seem to be going through a mental checklist so that we won't make fools of ourselves. And while we worry about being late or not properly prepared, we are likely to wake up before the alarm rings and have enough time to do all that is required for this event.

The amount of time spent dreaming varies from person to person and at different times of our lives. Infants spend most of their sleep time in REM—that is, in dreaming, which makes sense since dreams seem to facilitate learning. For infants, everything is new and they have more to learn from their daily lives than we do when we are older. As adults, we generally spend less and less time dreaming as we age. This will vary widely among individuals. (See chapter 2 for increasing dream recall.) Dreamtime can change dramatically during periods of illness or crisis when our dreaming and our recall will increase. If, in our later adult years, we take on a new and challenging project such as learning a foreign language, the time spent in REM sleep will also increase. Many of us have had the experience of learning a new task and then feeling as if we continued doing the same task all night in our dreams.

If you systematically and deliberately deprive people of dream sleep by waking them each time they go into REM, they become irritable and angry. When finally allowed to sleep and dream normally, they spend more than their usual time in REM sleep—almost as if they are compensating for the dreamtime they lost. If such deprivation is continued for a long period, these individuals begin to hallucinate even though they have no history of hallucination. One theory is that the hallucinations experienced by those who have been deprived of their dreams are now "awake dreams"—also a compensation for lost dreamtime. Note that alcohol and other tranquilizing drugs decrease dreaming.

Many dreams seem to be expressions of wishes and desires. One woman who dreamed of shopping for human organs in a supermarket where she could pick out a liver, pancreas, and new heart, was in the process of dealing with her father's diagnosis of terminal cancer. On the day before the dream, she had learned the cancer had spread to all his vital organs and in her dream she devised a way to solve this problem by just buying new body parts for him.

Our sexual dreams, which we will discuss at length in chapter 8, are also expressions of desires and wishes at times. At other times, they have other metaphorical meanings, as we shall see. All too often, the dreamer is stuck in the concrete images of the dream and has difficulty hearing the metaphor.

While some dreams are expressions of our wishes, they aren't always wishes. A dream about someone's death isn't necessarily a wish, though it could be. The dreamer will know whether she harbors feelings of such strong hostility toward the person who dies in the dream. The dream could just as easily express a fear of loss of this person. Or the dream might be telling the dreamer that something in him needs to die and that part is symbolized by the other person. To assume that all dreams are wishes and desires is to miss the many other possible layers of meanings in dreams.

One of the most impressive benefits of dreamwork is that dreams help us to solve our problems. We use the old adage "I need to sleep on it" before making some important decision. This sentiment seems to have some basis in reality. If we go to bed undecided or plagued by some problem, we might wake up with what appears to be a sponta- neous solution. While we were sleeping, our minds were busy work- ing and reworking the problem, making order of what seemed to be a mass of confusion when we closed our eyes. In fact, we can ask for solutions to our problems by going to bed with a question deliberately held in our minds. (See chapter 5 for dream incubation techniques.)

Another function of dreams is their ability to give us clarity. Not only do we see this in the problem-solving ability mentioned above, but we also see it in dreams that give us a more honest pic- ture of who we are. If I am telling myself that I'm a person who keeps her promises, the dream might remind me that I tried to back out of a commitment. Dreams will often find the discrepan- cies in my self-image and my behavior. One of the reasons why dreams are sometimes painful to look at is that even when we don't know what the dream means, we hesitate to remember it or tell it to another person because we feel anxious that we are going to find out something about ourselves we may not want to hear.

Getting past our resistance by working with dreams regularly, we are better able to embrace our dreams, including our night- mares, because we know how much valuable information is con- tained in them. The way we lie to ourselves or deny reality will come through in our dreams. The parts of myself I reject will flaunt themselves in my dreams. I may wake up feeling disturbed and un- comfortable with the dream I had, but I remind myself that when I get beyond that feeling there will be information in the dream that will be of help to me in more than one area of my life.

In one of my dreams, I am listening to a message on my telephone answering system. A woman I know is making a long speech to me, lecturing me about what I'm doing wrong, cataloguing my defects, and criticizing me. I am listening and becoming more and more upset and outraged that she's doing this. Who asked her? And what's worse, because she has left this message and not said this live, I can't interrupt, stop her, or defend myself. The message seems to go on and on. I see her as dominating, controlling, intrusive, and judging me harshly and without any understanding.

On waking, I was puzzled by this dream. I thought about the woman I know who left the message and she is only a peripheral person in my life, not someone I have much contact with. I find her a bit difficult to deal with. I find I shrink in her presence. She acts as if she knows everything. Her superior attitude is unhelpful and intimidating. But because I have little exposure to this person, I doubted she represented herself or my relationship with her on any significant level. Rather, I suspected she must be someone else in my life. That, too, didn't bring any feelings of having made a connection. I couldn't think of anyone in my life I'd interacted with in that way the day or two before the dream or who was on my mind the night before the dream who fit this description.

That meant the woman in the dream might be part of myself. To my dismay, exploring this layer brought a real sense of recognition. I immediately recognized myself as being the critical, lecturing, judgmental person. This was an accurate description of my behavior in a relatively new and fragile friendship. I had been finding fault with this friend, telling her what she should do, criticizing her choices and the way she was running her life and finances. While she had asked me for advice and feedback, I had given her much more than she had asked for. She had already complained about my tone and questions. I was treating her as if I were her mother—and not a very compassionate or empathetic mother, either. The dream, as all dreams do, told me something about myself that I needed to know. I was lying to myself in believing I was being nice to her with my concern, but the dream said I was being cruel in my criticism and that it would undo the friendship if I continued. With this insight, I immediately called her and told her the dream, explained what I thought it meant, and apologized for my insensitivity.

This opened a discussion between us that was a big improvement in our relationship. Now when she catches me lapsing into this pattern, she says, "Thank you, Mother," and we both laugh. The dream was a more honest picture of how I was coming across than I could see of myself in waking life. On another layer, this dream might be telling me how critical I am of myself.

Similarly, many people like to retain memories of their childhood as being a time of comfort, security, and trouble-free bliss. However, no one arrives at adulthood without wounds. Most of us have fears and traumas related to our past. This is especially true of childhood when we were poorly equipped to handle our experiences. In our dreams, we continue to work on past events, comparing them to present events and assimilating them over time. There are times in our lives when memories of past hurts and wounds will surface, often through our dreams. One explanation is that when we reach new levels of mental health and competence, we are better able to deal with what might have terrorized us at an earlier stage. The unconscious, by sending us a dream of a forgotten or repressed memory, is saying, "Okay, I'm giving you this now because you're ready to handle it." The dream opens the door to working with these issues on a conscious level, which we were previously unable to do. At this time, we may be ready to resolve old traumas. In psychological terms, we are now prepared to integrate them into our personalities instead of keeping them partitioned off or projected onto others.

DREAMS ARE NOT THE SAME AS MEMORIES

It is important to remember, however, that dreams that seem to take place in our childhood are not true memories or accurate representations of events that took place. Memory is not a perfect recording of events that remain intact, accurate, and whole some-where in our minds, as many people think. Rather, memories are a mixture of impressions and fuzzy recording, elaborated and changed over time and with each episode of recall and retelling. This latter process is referred to as confabulation and accounts for some of the differences between reports of evidence presented in a court of law (Loftus and Ketchum, 1991; Terr, 1994). Dreams may be traces of memories of past events, but they are more often cre-ative metaphors about our present lives. In responding to a question about whether a trauma victim would have dreams about the event, Lenore Terr, M.D., writes, "While I acknowledged that dreams are important to trauma, I added that dreams are not always connected to trauma. Children do not necessarily dream about their traumas. Nor, by the time they reach adulthood, do childhood trauma victims necessarily start dreaming. Some people who repress do dream, par-ticularly as their memories begin to come back toward the surface. But many such people do not" (1994).

If you ever tried to compare your experience of a childhood event (even a nontraumatic or happy one) with a sibling, you will discover the enormous differences between how each of you re-members the experience, and the way you processed its meaning.

Yapko (1994) warns of the dangers of therapist influence in cases of suspected abuse and how we should not rely on dreams as a factual source for verifying suspicions of abuse. Clients in therapy are suggestible and eager for relief. They want an explanation for their distressing symptoms and problems. Dreams are not memo-ries. They are dreams—with all the distortions and impressionistic and creative imagery that dreams offer. To assume that a dream is the same as a memory or a confirmation of a memory can be a dan-gerously inaccurate examination of reality.

However, dreams can also be a vehicle for resolving our prob-lems and traumas. One woman, whom I'll call "Cindy," brought a dream to a workshop in which she looks in the mirror and finds her hair is all stiff and spiky rather than soft and fluffy the way it usually is. Cindy can't understand how this has happened. In the next scene, she is at the beauty salon. As soon as she sits down, the hairdresser, who is Audrey Hepburn, rips a toupee off Cindy's head. Underneath, Cindy's scalp is raw, sore, and bloody. Cindy is appalled at this. In her dream, she wonders, "How could I have been wearing this toupee all this time and not even know it?" And her head hurts when her scalp is exposed. She titled this dream "Cindy Rubbed Raw."

In working with this dream, I asked for details, a description of a toupee (notice she didn't say wig), and about Audrey Hepburn. I asked her what her feelings were in the dream and how she felt when she woke up. Then I asked Cindy when she had the dream. She had been on a visit with her husband to see her parents, and she said the visit was particularly difficult for her. This was the first time she had seen her parents since she had confronted her father about his abuse. Being with them again, she feared she would slip back into her old passive ways of interacting with them, which she hoped she had changed. Seeing her parents again also brought up a lot of old issues including exposing her wounds once more.

Cindy was able to bridge this dream to waking life. She could see that wearing a toupee was a false self she had worn for years for her parents, that underneath it were the wounds she still had and they still hurt. In the dream, she didn't even realize she had been wearing this toupee. This validated the work she was doing with her therapist about how she hadn't been true or honest with herself in the years she participated in the family lies. That way of being had become so comfortable, she didn't even know it wasn't her, just as she didn't know she'd been wearing a toupee.

Audrey Hepburn's appearance is no accident, either. At the time of this dream, Cindy was still struggling with an eating disorder and strongly identified with Hepburn's appearance. At the same time, Cindy admired her as a beautiful, proper woman. Certainly, calling the hairpiece a toupee could be explored in terms of Cindy's masculine side.

Perhaps you've thought of other explanations and approaches to this dream. There is no real end to working with dreams because they are layered with meanings.

Another woman woke from a dream feeling very upset and disturbed. In this dream, "Diane" is having an argument with a man. She is so angry that she hits him and he falls to the ground, injuring his foot. Then she kneels to help him. As she tries to see the extent of his wound, she is unable to get his shoe off. Every time she looks, she discovers she's tied his shoelaces into more and more knots instead of untying them, which is what she intended. Diane found this dream very disturbing. She would never hit anyone and she felt terrible discovering that she was tying knots in the man's shoelaces when he needed medical attention. It was not in keeping with her waking image of herself.

Can you hear the metaphor?

I asked Diane about the waking events of her day, and she'd had a conflict with a woman at work. They were in a dispute about a procedure. I said, "In the dream, you are making knots even though you're trying to untie the laces. In what way might you be making things worse at work while you are trying to make them better?" Diane leaped out of her chair and wanted to make a phone call. This was an *aha* if ever I saw one. I encouraged her to wait while we discussed the details and what the dream might be saying. Clearly, Diane saw that she was, indeed, making things worse. The next day, she was able to have a talk with her co-worker and resolve the problem to her satisfaction. Diane was amazed at how clearly the dream had given her the message of how she was messing up.

DREAMS AS PROPHECY

One of the most frequently asked questions about the function of dreaming is whether dreams warn us about the future. Are dreams prophecy? Do they come to us so that we can avert danger?

I believe dreams often appear to be a prophecy because we are aware at a deeper level of our being (call it unconscious or subconscious or in our heart and soul) of where our present path will lead us. If we continue our behaviors in our relationships, at work, or in the way we care for our bodies, we know what the outcome will be. If you arrive at work late and leave work early every day, your prophecy of getting fired and seeing it happen in the dream is not a surprise.

If you are abusing your body with drugs, alcohol, insufficient sleep, and poor nutrition, then having dreams about your own death or illness is not simply a prediction of the future. Rather, you are alerting yourself of the need to make a change in your life. These dream warnings might come as you begin to be aware of a deterioration in your physical health, the security of your job, or the stability of your relationships. I believe that dreamwork with these early dreams of problems can help us avoid the serious consequences of a path we are on before it is too late to make changes. Certainly, if couples share their dreams on a regular basis, the first indications of difficulties in communication and trust will be evident in the dream and can be addressed before they become so angry with each other that intimacy and repairing damage in the relationship become close to impossible.

DREAMS AS MEMORIES OF PAST LIVES

Many people want to know whether dreams are memories of past lives. For those who believe in past lives, this is a serious question. One's cosmology or view of how the universe works will impact on both the content of dreams and on how the dreamer will interpret them. If a dreamer tells me this is a past-life memory, I remind her that the dream must also be a source of useful and current information. The dreamer's temptation is to explore this past life, find out about it, look for means to verify the validity of the experiences. In a way, this could be used as a way to reenter the believed past life rather than living in the present one.

We have our dreams at a particular time because they have use for us; they are message-bringers. As with any dream of old memories (from this lifetime or whenever), I ask, Why now? What is the dream telling you about your life that you need to know now? How is this useful information?

Certainly, if we have had past lives and find ourselves in the world again, we can still learn from those previous lifetimes. Dreams are not just movies to entertain us—though they are often entertaining. They come with a message for today's life in today's world. Ask yourself, "How is this a Teaching for me right now? What action is the dream pointing me toward?"

DREAMS AND ILLNESS

Some people believe that dreams can help us in diagnosing possible physical illnesses. Dreams about our bodies or about houses as representations of the body may help us know where we are ill and what part of our bodies need special care. Once again, we must look at information we see in a dream by using the power of our conscious minds and practical knowledge to evaluate the accuracy of such information. The dream may be only a red flag suggesting further investigation by medical professionals. I would not rely on a dream about my physical health as the only source of information on my body's well-being, but I would take heed if a dream seemed to indicate an illness. I would confirm or refute my suspicions by seeing a doctor for a checkup.

Ultimately, the function of dreaming seems to be to make conscious what is unconscious: that is, to make us aware of what we already know at some deeper level. This information that comes to consciousness is often valuable and useful in a practical way, as the many examples in this book will illustrate.

two

Dream Recall: How It Works

MANY PEOPLE FIND THE IDEA OF DREAMWORK interesting but say they don't remember their dreams. "I never dream," they say, or "I don't remember my dreams." This message, sent to the unconscious every time it is stated, is a powerful one. If we tell ourselves we can't do something—anything—then we can be certain this will be so. If you are someone who doesn't remember your dreams except on rare occasions, I would suggest you stop telling yourself you don't remember them. A desire to remember and a willingness to be open to the content of the dream is the first step to improving recall.

Everyone dreams every night, even though we remember only a small fraction of our dreams. Even experienced dreamworkers will have days or weeks when they don't remember a dream. At best, we remember only a portion of a dream life; most of it passes through our minds with little notice. It is usually the impact of an emotional dream that awakens us. Or a strong or disturbing image might linger after we wake.

All of us have had the experience of forgetting our dreams.

How often have you awakened and remembered a dream with the intent of telling it to someone, only to have it disappear within a few minutes of rising? You are sure you'll remember, but when you try to recite the dream, it's gone—melted away. Evaporated. Stephen King says dreams decompose. Maybe they just float away.

WHY WE DON'T REMEMBER OUR DREAMS

There are many reasons we don't remember our dreams, some of which are a result of our culture's attitude toward dreams, and some because of the personal feelings we bring to the content of our dreams and what they reveal about the inner workings of our minds.

Our culture doesn't honor dreams. We're told from childhood, "Oh, it was just a dream," which trivializes the experience and dismisses the emotions attached as too unimportant to explore or understand. For some, dreams are scary and embarrassing, and we'd rather forget them. Their memory raises uncomfortable or painful feelings we would prefer to avoid. Many of us fear the content of dreams exposes aspects of ourselves we don't want to know or acknowledge. The violence, raw sexuality, and bizarre composition make us wonder if these images might be evidence of mental illness. We might dream of shooting people or of cutting off our own arms. Fragments of such dreams make us wish we didn't remember them, often pushing them out of our consciousness. We don't want to tell our dreams to others who might think we're crazy, weird, or dangerous.

Sometimes we would prefer not to know them ourselves, fearing that they will tell us things about ourselves we'd prefer to leave buried. Our nightmares scare us and call up feelings we don't like: terror, panic, and impending doom and death. And, since dreams are occasionally prophetic, we fear the events in them might come true. At these times, we need to remind ourselves that all dreams are gifts. Your dreams, no matter how troubling, are normal for you and will help you when you take the time to look at them more closely for their meanings and messages. Try to remember that when you get to the other side of any dream, you will have a different perspective on it and will no longer feel upset by it.

If you leap out of bed in the morning to the sound of a clock radio or alarm, it's likely you won't remember your dreams. In our busy society, most of us immediately start thinking about what we have to do for the day ahead instead of thinking about where we've been in our dream world. As soon as we start thinking about where we have to be and what we have to do, the dream is gone.

When we do remember a dream and begin to tell it to our mates or co-workers, we are likely to be met with teasing, scorn, or indifference. Other people's dreams seem boring. Most people won't be interested in our dreams because they don't know the value of them. Our wanting to tell the dream to someone else is often a result of our strong sense that the dream contains important information if we could only understand the images from this weird kingdom.

Another reason we might not remember our dreams is the mistaken belief by some that doing dreamwork is entering dangerous territory. Maybe it's the dark side, the other side where spirits live, or the occult. Such myths keep us from exploring ourselves and benefiting from the abundance of helpful information dreams provide. Each time I look at a dark dream of my own or someone else's, I am in awe of how much wisdom, insight, and creativity is beneath the grotesque images.

WAYS TO IMPROVE DREAM RECALL

Clearly, you can't work with your dreams unless you can remember them. First, you must decide that you want to remember them. Begin by telling yourself you will remember a dream on waking. Often, just thinking about dreams and having a conversation about them causes people to remember a dream for the first time in a long while. Many people who come to my lectures will remember a dream the next morning— especially those who don't ordinarily remember their dreams. By attending and listening to the value of dreams, they have sent a message to their unconscious of their interest in dreams. They wake up with a dream recalled.

Remembering dreams takes more than desire, however. It takes a commitment to do the steps that help to remember. I, too, won't remember my dreams unless I use all the aids to remembering.

• 12 STEPS TO RECALL YOUR DREAMS •

1. Keep a notebook and pen ready at your bedside. If you have a sleeping partner, you can tape a penlight to a ballpoint pen so you don't have to use a bright light to record your dream. Some people prefer a handheld or voice-activated tape recorder.

2. As you go to sleep, imagine yourself writing your dreams when you wake up.

3. Tell yourself you WILL remember a dream in the morning.

4. Whenever possible, try not to use alarms or clock radios to avoid their jarring effects. For this reason, days off and vacations are good times to capture dreams.

5. Avoid the use of alcohol and tranquilizers, both of which inhibit dreaming and dream recall. This is equally true of narcotics and some hallucinogenic drugs. Some medications such as antipsychotics and relaxers will also reduce dreaming or dream recall; others can cause nightmares. *Always consult your physician before discontinuing or changing the dosage of any prescription drugs.* Increasing the intake of Vitamins B-6 and C increases dream recall for some individuals.

6. When you wake up, try to stay in the same physical position in bed. Instead of jumping up to begin your day, remain still and ask yourself what you were just thinking about. Try asking yourself: Where was I? What was just happening? What am I feeling now? Go over the dream several times in your mind to memorize the events no matter how nonsensical or disturbing.

7. Record, in writing or on tape, the entire dream with every detail you can remember. Capture the setting, characters, time of day, physical sensations, emotional tone, dialogue, animals, actions of the dream, colors, smells, and how the dream ends. Nothing is trivial.

Let me say that again. No detail in a dream is trivial and no dream is trivial, though there are some that have more information than others.

8. Write down whatever comes to mind even if it seems completely senseless and bizarre. A few notes are better than nothing. A fragment of a dream when recorded and reviewed will often bring back an entire dream. Dream fragments by themselves can be loaded with information. Rather than dismissing them as incomplete, think of them as perfect little poems—with all the flavor and richness of a haiku.

A dreamer shared, "Toothbrush in hand, I scrub away all traces of my guilty pleasure."

9. If you have no dream to write down, at least record the feelings and thoughts you have when you wake up. Doing this regularly will open the doorway to remembering dreams.

10. Try drinking a large amount of water before bedtime. (This is not recommended for children or the elderly.) When you wake up to use the bathroom, you might capture what you were dreaming. If you do, make some notes. A few key words or phrases are often enough to help you recall your

dream in the morning. Don't assume you'll remember your dream without making notes. You probably won't.

11. Get into the habit of giving your dreams titles. Choose a title that evokes some of the imagery and feeling of the dream. Instead of calling a dream "The Scary Animal," you might want to call it "Bear in the Closet," which will make it more specific. This will help you to refer to them as well as helping you to remember them. Looking at a list of titles over time is a good way to pick up themes and to see your personal evolution.

12. Be patient and keep trying. The more you want to remember your dreams and the more you pay attention to the ones you have, the more dreams you'll remember. When you have too many to record and work on, commit to working on at least one dream per week in detail.

One more suggestion: If possible, choose a notebook that pleases you. Having a beautiful book and a special pen to record your dreams tells your unconscious that you value your dreams. Honoring them in this way adds to your ability to recall dreams and to your attitude about working with them. You might even want to add drawings, artwork, or colorful designs on the cover or to each of the dreams. These efforts give dreams the reverence they deserve.

THE ORDER OF REMEMBERED DREAMS: WHICH ONE CAME FIRST?

When remembering dreams, it is frequently difficult to know for sure which one came first. Was one scene before another, or did it come after? Did I have this dream early in the evening or later than the one I remembered first? Does it matter?

In general, it doesn't matter in what order you tell or remember a dream. Dreams have an out-of-time quality, with all the events seeming to occur simultaneously. For us to recall and begin doing dreamwork, we must tell them in some kind of order as if there were a true chronology to the dream. Speech is linear, so we convert the dream into a linear format, but that's only to make it available for further exploration. The order doesn't matter because you will look at each scene and each dream of a sequence as one whole when you are done looking at the parts. The summary conclusions and interpretations will be what matters, not the order in which they came to you. So don't fret about trying to remember the dream in the "right" order.

WHAT DREAMS BRING US

Our emotions are laid bare in our sleep. We see the raw aggression and rage in us, the unchecked and indiscriminate sexuality. The grief we thought was past rises again as do the hurts and wounds of childhood. In dream sleep, we can't stuff down the feelings the way we do in waking life when we distract ourselves or suppress the feelings with denial, drugs, alcohol, food, sex. Do you talk on the telephone a lot? Watch television? Work to exhaustion? Stay busy all the time? People use all kinds of means to keep from letting their feelings be part of their awareness. In dreams, the emotions are all there. The lid is off.

Even if we do remember a dream and want to tell it to someone—because we know instinctively that telling a dream is the first step toward discovering its meaning—those around us are frequently too busy to listen. They, too, are part of the culture that doesn't think dreams mean much. Dreams are relegated to that far-out business and are dismissed as fanciful at best. Or, they are considered to be phenomena only psychiatrists, psychics, and other "experts" can interpret. Not heard, our dreams don't get the kind of care and attention they need to reveal their meaning to us.

And once more, they're gone—evaporated into the universe or dispersed like a whiff of smoke.

Dreams are difficult to remember. I find it difficult even though I've been working with my dreams for many years. Because dreams don't come to us the way waking thoughts do, they are harder to remember and tell. They seem like jumbles of images and ideas without any waking logic or sense. Trying to tell a dream we do remember is often an effort. We must convert the simultaneous, confusing events and pictures into a linear, chronological order to catch the dream. We are more likely to remember the dreams that terrify, repulse, puzzle, or leave us sexually aroused. Most dreams are not emotionally charged at all, so they fade from consciousness quickly.

People work with their dreams—believe in them, you might say—because those who have attended to their dreams know how helpful they can be. Each day, our dreams are telegrams sent from ourselves to ourselves. Contained in the dream is a statement about our current situation—often in every important area in our lives.

The Talmud tells us an uninterpreted dream is like an unopened letter. For those who want to do inner work, this is an excellent route to the core of who we are. Dreams reveal our truest selves without all the props and masks we've learned to wear.

In our dreams, we are more honest than when we are awake. We tell ourselves the truth about ourselves, our relationships, our strengths, and our weaknesses. We evaluate our work and our loves, the ways in which we cheat or feel we have been cheated. If you have a dream of seeing yourself or someone else stealing at work, you might ask how you are stealing in a metaphoric way. Maybe you tell yourself you're working hard, but you always arrive late. Dreams give us an opposing and compensating view when we see the world or ourselves as too rosy or not rosy enough. Sometimes when we have been very critical of someone whom we dislike intensely we will have a dream about making love to this person. We wake up appalled at the idea. But the dream is adding balance to our lives, telling us there is another way to look at this person. It may be saying that we have this person inside us, as part of us. Perhaps this individual represents part of ourselves that we deny.

Each dream can be seen as a snapshot of where we are on the day of the dream. It is a status report without the rose-colored glasses, excuses, and rationalizations to which we are all prone. Though we may choose to gloss over those moments of anger and outrage, erotic urges, or feelings of fear and inadequacy, the dream brings them back to us—often in an exaggerated and dramatic form—as though the dream were trying to scream some important information into our awareness and waking consciousness.

Jeremy Taylor, in *Where People Fly and Water Runs Uphill* (1992), reminds us that dreams come to tell us what we don't already know. This is a paradox; we know something on one level of consciousness, but not on another. In our dreams, we know about ourselves and others in a way that is often not available when we are awake. This unconscious level includes intellectual, emotional, psychological, physical, and spiritual awareness. Our dreams bring us new information—information we need to know but already have on a deeper, unconscious level. This is the kind of knowledge we're aware of through our intuitions, feelings, or what some people call "vibes" about others or our surroundings. The dream helps to bring these facts and impressions to full, mindful awareness.

Let us look at one dream as an example. A woman dreams she is trying to put in a contact lens. The lens is huge—larger than her whole face. Holding it in the palm of her hand, she raises it toward her face and brings it back down again, aware that she can't make it fit her eye. Connecting the dream to waking life, the woman said she had just been promoted on her job. While she consciously told herself she could meet her new responsibilities and she denied any anxiety, her dream seemed to say that on another level she felt her promotion was too big for her. The feelings in the dream were not greatly anxious, however. What the dream told her was that her voiced feelings were not the whole story. In fact, she did feel a bit stressed-out over this advancement. The dream gave her an opportunity to explore whether she had taken on something bigger than she could handle or whether it was simply an expression of feelings she hadn't let herself be aware of. The dream balanced her waking beliefs.

At another level, this dream was also about her primary personal relationship, giving clarity to another area of her life. We explored how this relationship didn't fit her eye—perhaps her mind's eye, of what the relationship should be. This was hardly more than a dream fragment, but it contains many messages for the dreamer.

WHAT TO DO WHEN YOU HAVE TOO MANY DREAMS

Some people complain they wake up every day with many remembered dreams. They are numerous, vivid, long, and complicated. How does one begin to work with this flood of information?

If you are in this position of having many, many dreams, consider yourself privileged. Your unconscious is working overtime to tell you what you need to know, and you have ready access to this information. Rather than trying to record all the dreams and all the details, choose those that stand out in your mind because they have the most vivid imagery and the strongest feelings. Record nightmares because they can be the most helpful. When the images are upsetting and offensive, these are the dreams that may be the best gifts from your unconscious. Record a few of these vivid dreams and choose to work on at least one per week in detail. That means taking the time to write it down as completely as possible and follow the steps discussed in this book to uncover the meanings of the dream, knowing there will be more than one meaning in these intense dreams.

Trying to record and do dreamwork on all your dreams is an unrealistic and impossible task. You won't have time to do anything else. Don't turn the joyous discovery and puzzle-piecing of dreamwork into a chore or another pile of unfinished drudgery. If you work on a few dreams in detail, you will get the messages you need to know. Many dreams are repeat messages given to you in other dreams. This is especially true of dreams from the same evening or dreams you remember together or want to tell together. Working on one of them can be extremely helpful. It isn't necessary to work on all of them. Often, working on one dream in detail, especially the last one of the night, will help you with quickly understanding the other dreams since the themes and messages are often related. You might want to commit to working on one dream a week in detail, perhaps spending an hour or so on a vivid, clear dream.

OLD DREAMS, DREAMS OF THE REMEMBERED PAST

I generally encourage people to bring current dreams to work with. I ask, "Who has a dream hot off the pillow?" knowing we will be able to get a lot more information from a recent dream where the associations are still fresh and pertinent to the here and now. Because it is current, the dreamer has the opportunity to use this information immediately. Even better is a nightmare that woke the dreamer and left him feeling uneasy or fearful. At workshops, I always ask for nightmares and recurrent dreams first.

However, many people have a dream they had years ago—as many as twenty or thirty years ago—that still stands out in their minds. The images and feelings are as vivid as if they were from the night before.

A dream remembered for many years probably holds special significance. Getting to the meaning is more difficult, however.

Since the dream was a current status report at the time of the dream, I ask, When did the dream take place? What was going on in your life at that time?

With these Big Dreams, as some call them, the dreamer can often remember what was happening at the time of the dream. Frequently, some crisis in the person's life will be recalled: a traumatic event of some kind such as a death or divorce, a serious illness for the dreamer or someone close to him. It may have taken place during a particularly trying time in childhood—a change of home and school, perhaps. Maybe the dreamer experienced the death or loss of a beloved pet. Or it was the year the dreamer's mother had a miscarriage, which he didn't understand as a child.

Working with an old dream can be helpful. The dreamer's urgency to talk about the dream and the associated events can lead to some new understanding and resolution. A childhood crisis will look very different through adult eyes. But much about the dream may remain a mystery. We don't have the child here to associate to the images and symbols of the dream. We have an adult whose life experiences will change the way those images are seen.

At the same time, an urgency to tell an old dream may indicate that the dream has meaning today.

WHY IS IT THAT SO MANY DREAMS ARE BAD DREAMS?

In fact, many of our dreams are bland and unemotional. People who recall many dreams find only some of them to be frightening or disturbing. Many are just puzzling or exotic images. Most dreams go unremembered. Out of the six or more dreams we have each night, rarely will more than three be recalled—even by those people who recall many dreams. We are most likely to remember those whose images and actions are charged with strong emotions. We remember the ones that woke us up terrified, or left us sexually aroused. We remember the dreams of our own violence to others or the threat of violence or loss to ourselves. Studies have shown that strong emotion, whether in sleep or in waking life, promotes the retention of a memory. That's why the memories of a single trauma may be burned in our brains forever. You probably forget many of your day-to-day ordinary activities. If I ask you what you did last Monday afternoon, you have likely forgotten unless it was an event that made you react with powerful emotions. If you had a car accident, were a witness to an assault, took your first sky-diving lesson, or fell in love, you would be more likely to remember.

Many common dreams have powerful feelings and are easily remembered. These may be dreams of being chased, falling, flying, plane crashes, or being in public without clothing. We'll discuss common dreams and common dream themes, including some pleasant ones, in chapter 9.

If you believe you are not remembering your dreams because you wake up often during the night or because you aren't getting enough sleep to dream, see suggestions in Appendix P for dealing with insomnia.

When you begin doing dreamwork by remembering dreams, you'll find yourself able to recognize some dream meanings almost immediately. Keep in mind, though, that the meaning that is closest to the surface is usually not the dream's most important message. That is only the first layer. It's the layer we already know consciously. Working further, especially with others, we are pushed a bit to probe to a deeper level, to look for the information in the dream that is new. When people say they know the meaning of a dream because it's obvious, I say, "That's layer one." I encourage them to look beyond the obvious. Working regularly on dreams with friends or in a dream group helps us to do this. (See chapter 6 for working on your dreams in groups or with a dream partner.)

·*three*·

What Do Dreams Mean?

YOU HAVE A REMEMBERED DREAM AND YOU haven't the slightest idea what it means. Further, you're not sure you want to know. If you're like most people, the thought of sharing your dreams with others or deciphering their symbols raises some anxiety. Uh-oh, you may think, what's going to come out of this one?

I confess, I often have the same feeling. Even after working with my dreams for years and truly believing they are always gifts—including the nightmares—I feel edgy before telling a dream to my dream partner or in front of a group. However, I know that dreams are *always* a source of important information and listening to the message can save me some time. In a few months, the dream's meaning may be clear to me. But right now, if I take the time to heed the significance of the dream, I might save myself some trouble and worry.

To find out what their dreams mean, some people look up the key words in a dream dictionary. Others go to dream experts and ask something like: I had a dream about a house with blue walls. What does that mean?

I don't tell people what their dreams mean. I may have a good guess, an educated guess, perhaps, but I also know how often I can be wrong. Anything I say about another's dream can only be my own projection of the issues I am dealing with personally. The same is true for anything said by anyone else. These projections are sometimes helpful to the dreamer, but only after he has had an opportunity to come up with his own interpretations and see how the dream relates to his current life situations.

Only the dreamer knows what a dream means. My function is to help the dreamer by asking the right questions so the metaphor will be discovered. The dreamer then makes a bridge to his waking life. Or he relates the dream to an important event in his past that connects with some event in the present. Keep in mind that no matter what the setting or time frame of the dream, it is always about what is current in your life. It may also be about past or future events, but primarily, it is about the present.

Without looking up your dream in a dictionary or asking someone what it means, there are *many* ways to get to the meaning.

All dreams come to us in the language of metaphor and symbol. Some people believe the symbols we use are chosen to disguise their meaning—as if we were trying to evade or avoid the meaning of the dream. In my experience of working with my own and others' dreams, I am in agreement with modern dreamworkers who believe the dream symbols we choose are the best ones possible to convey the message of the dream to ourselves. Similar to the use of images and metaphor in poetry and fiction, we choose a symbol as a way to say something most directly with an economy of words. And, like poetry, a dream has layers of meaning. The play of words is intricate at the same time that it is precise, punning, and playful.

One man dreamed of a bull who was out to kill him. Later in the dream, the bull turned into a man. When asked for a description of the bull, he said it was a strong, dangerous animal, but it could sometimes be gentle and kind. Immediately, he realized that the bull depicted the best and worst aspects of his father's personality. At another level, the dream was about his concerns on his job and his boss—another bull in his life. For the play on words, he realized that both of these authority figures gave him a lot of bull.

There are many different ways to work with dreams to get to their meaning. I use a variety of techniques depending on the content of the dream and the personality and awareness of the dreamer. I also consider the overall mood of my interaction with the dreamer and her reaction to her dream. The setting of the dreamwork, too, might be a deciding factor about choice of technique. In a private setting, we might be more likely to act out part of the dream or discuss personal associations that might not be easily shared in a larger group.

When working with someone's dream, I first ask him to tell the dream uninterrupted from start to finish. While listening, I pay attention to my feelings as well as my own thoughts and associations. In a group, I encourage the others to listen to the recounting of the dream on more than an intellectual or cognitive level. The aim is for us to experience the dream along with the dreamer—as if it were our dream.

After the dream has been told from start to finish, we go back over it. I ask for clarification, trying to see each image and scene clearly. In particular, I am alert to the dreamer's feelings throughout the dream, which will help us to identify the possible meanings. I ask for descriptions of each image even when the dream is of something familiar to me. This is especially important because my assumptions about an image, place, or animal are frequently very different from those of the dreamer. One woman described a fox as cuddly and friendly. That surprised me and reminded me to leave my assumptions aside when first working with someone else's dream.

At the end of the first telling of the dream, I ask the dreamer why she thinks she had the dream. "What might the dream be trying to tell you?" I ask. "How do the feelings of the dream sound like the feelings you had on the day you had the dream?"

Then we examine each of the elements of the dream. Some of the elements are:

place or setting
actions
strongest emotions
theme or major idea
images
character(s), animals
sounds, rhythm
sensations
texture or touch
dialogue, conversation
messages, phrases, or single words
movement or physical orientation
smells
tastes
dream title

I encourage the dreamer to give a summary of the dream in one or two sentences, which usually helps her to hear the metaphor. Remember, only the dreamer knows the true meaning or meanings of the dream.

As an example, let us explore a woman's dream in which she found a dog in her house. Knowing that her feelings about dogs and mine might be completely at odds, I ask her to tell me about dogs and about this specific dream dog. What does it look like? Because I know this dog and the events of the dream are metaphors for this woman's present life situation, while she's describing her dream dog, I listen for other possible meanings, including puns, homonyms, and figures of speech.

Think a moment about how you might describe a dog. What comes to your mind? What breed do you see? What memories of dogs past and present come up for you? What does the dog in your imagination do? You might want to close your eyes for a minute and see where the thought of dogs leads you. Take a few moments to consider your associations of dogs past and present.

In answer to my question about dogs, the dreamer says they are "big, ferocious, and unpredictable." In a moment, she adds: "They are messy and a big bother." A dog would tie her down, restrict her freedom.

I have two dogs and while I can understand her point of view, none of these adjectives would be the first to come to *my* mind. I'd be more inclined to describe dogs as loving, loyal, and devoted— even protective. For me, they are a comfort because my love is always accepted.

Certainly, the word DOG calls up radically different thoughts and feelings for each of us. Her description is the only one that counts right now since this is HER dream: a message from herself to herself.

As part of the dreamwork, I will repeat key phrases and expressions that the dreamer used while telling the dream and giving descriptions, using the dreamer's own words. Upon repeating her description of the dog, she will often hear something else. She laughs first and then says, "That sounds like my boss." Or my father, or my husband or my project at work, she might have said— using this dog to symbolize someone or something in her life. "Big, unpredictable, and messy," she repeats. I can see she has made a connection.

"And a bother?" I ask. "That, too," she answers and she throws her head back and laughs. "Ferocious?" I ask. "Yes!" she says, "He can be such a bear!"—and we both laugh at this second animal metaphor.

People ask me how I know when a valid meaning has been reached. Usually, it's unquestionable. Though it may be only one of several accurate meanings, you will know when you hit on one when it's your dream. You have a sense of all the details fitting together. If you are observing someone else in a dream group, you will recognize the laugh or blush that comes at the instant of understanding. This is the true *aha* for a dream. It is physical as well as intellectual. They throw their heads back and laugh, or they cover their faces with their hands. They *know* when the meaning is right for them and you will see it in their bodies.

However, this doesn't always happen. Sometimes, the meaning eludes the dreamer. Perhaps it is because of a blind spot, which we all have. The dreamer may be not quite ready to fully grasp the dream's meaning. On subsequent nights, the dreamer might ask herself to dream other dreams with a request for clarification. Or the meaning of the dream will be clearer a few days or months later. Some more-introverted individuals need more time alone to digest their dreamwork.

In some ways, this demonstrates how dreams seem to be ahead of our conscious minds—another way of saying that we have knowledge at a deeper, unconscious level. Because each of us has blind spots, we are often unable or unwilling to see the reality of a situation until some time has passed. A dream that appears nonsensical or bizarre may suddenly be understandable a few weeks later.

Later we might say, "I knew it all along," or "I had a bad feeling about this months ago," yet we weren't ready to take action. Maybe we want to wait and see. We hope things will get better, that people won't disappoint us or betray us. We hope that if we wait, the problem will go away. Most of the time, this desire is at a less-than-conscious level. In our dreams, we strip away these falsehoods and take off our rose-colored glasses. We see things as they truly are without rationalizations. In waking life, we sometimes see things as worse than they are and then the dream compensates by letting us know things aren't as bad as we thought.

I believe this is the reason that dreams so often appear prophetic. Some dreams may truly be prophetic in terms of predicting future events. But more often, I think we have picked up subtle clues, information that we don't register consciously, and these are played out in our dreams. We might predict accidents and illnesses because we have subliminally registered the information that points to their inevitability. Maybe we were aware of a change in voice quality on a telephone call. At the end of my mother's life, I could tell how she was feeling just by the way she said hello. One word was enough.

If we are vaguely aware that someone's health is deteriorating, we may dream about his or her death. When it happens, we think our dream was a prediction.

However, I want to stress that dreams about death are nearly always a metaphor of transformation and change rather than a prediction of real death. If we dream of our own death, this often refers to death in a symbolic way. Some part of us needs to die in order for us to grow. As we mature, take responsibility for our lives, and give up the old excuses and fears that have held us back, we are also giving up the familiar parts of ourselves. If we get divorced, change jobs, achieve promotions, or move to a better home, our equilibrium is disturbed. These can be scary events, even if we desire them and have worked toward them. A part of us feels the change as akin to death, and we literalize the image in our dreams.

One myth is if you dream of your own death, and you die in the dream, you will die in fact and not wake up. I don't know how this idea became part of our cultural beliefs about dreams. If someone dreamed of his death and then died in the dream, how would anyone else know? We all need to use more of our common sense when working with dreams. Obviously, many, many people have had dreams of dying and didn't die.

Rather than trying to determine if a dream is prophecy or metaphor, the best dreamwork is done by coming to a dream knowing that it will be layered with meanings. It may not be either/or but both.

Every dream is rich with information. No detail is trivial, nor is any dream trivial or unimportant. Every dream is rich with information. A woman who dreamed she bought three bananas on the way to the bus stop with her ex-husband was more concerned with the later details of the dream in which her husband was run over by a bus. When asked about the three bananas, she didn't see the significance of the number three.

Having established that one rotten banana was her ex-husband, I wondered who the other two men might be. As she talked about how her marriage was deteriorating, she revealed that she had previously married and divorced this man's older brother. I asked if there was another man in her life at the time of the dream, but she said no. Further discussion revealed her sexual involvement with all three brothers in this family. With an audible gasp, the entire workshop had an *aha* as we realized she had been involved with a bunch of rotten bananas. She had picked the perfect image to describe this family and her relationship to them. The sexuality contained in the choice of a banana was not lost on the group. She confirmed this by saying her husband had withheld sex as a punishment.

In this dreamwork, we focused on the woman's feelings toward the men in her life, and we saw her ex-husband who was run over by a bus as himself. We could peel away more layers of this dream and ask how she might see herself as a banana or a rotten banana. We could look at how she might be the bus driver wanting to run over her ex-husband, who was blocking the way—or how she is blocking her own progress by acting stubbornly as her ex-husband did. What part of herself has she projected onto her ex-husband? We might even ask how this relates to her work, her relationship with her friends, her relationship with herself, and her spiritual growth. All these questions are worthy of exploration.

Asking about our projections or how each element of the dream is a part of ourselves is a valuable approach, but as a sole method, it might miss the insights our dreams have about other people in our lives whom we are not seeing realistically.

If I go out with a friend and then dream that he has broken into my house, I will ask myself what my dream might be telling me about this person. In what way do I feel he has broken in? Does this refer to breaking into me as a person or into my belongings? Do I feel the person can't be trusted or is a thief? Or is this a metaphor for my feeling that he has intruded in a more psychological or emotional way? Similarly, if I dream of being raped, I would want to ask myself how I have been raped by this person. It may be psychological or emotional rape. Or how have I felt screwed over? Since our language uses these terms metaphorically, we may turn them into literal events in our dreams.

In the dream of finding a friend breaking into my house, I first examine the layers of the dream where I treat this man on the *object* level since he is a real person in my life. Then I might want to also look at how this person breaking into my house is a part of me, projected onto another: the *subject* level. How did this intrusion feel? If I felt threatened, I might ask myself in what ways I am being a threat to myself. What risky behavior does this dream point up? Is this a dream to warn me to be more cautious? Am I exposing myself to being robbed or robbing myself of something? If the dream figure stole something, what was stolen would be significant. Theft of my purse might mean my identity more than my money since I don't usually carry cash.

If the person was a faceless stranger, a shadowy person, or someone I felt I didn't know, then I would assume it is a figure on the subject level; that is, a part of me. My description of the person, his or her behavior, and my feelings toward him or her reveals information about that split-off part of myself.

After examining specific descriptions and details of the dream, we look at how they are relevant in the dreamer's current life. Remember, the dream is always a status report, a snapshot of the situation as it is right now. That means it may be skewed in some way (by giving an exaggerated picture), but it will often balance the dreamer's current conscious feelings and thoughts. The dreamer will often be able to make a bridge to waking life and the issues that are of most interest.

Then we look at how the dream is a metaphor for each of our life concerns: in terms of the relationship to—
a mate, lover, or spouse
a friend or several friends
work and co-workers
self—that is, in terms of our inner life and psychological growth
our bodies and our health

We might add, on a Transpersonal scale, the more expansive dimensions of relationship to nature, one's community, the planet, and our spiritual life as we define it (God, the Life Force, or the Universe).

The dream may—and often does—have layers of meaning on each of these levels. As we asked in the woman's dream about the bananas, we can always find more information if we take the time to look for it. *Feelings* in dreams are one of the keys to their meaning. I will often ask a dreamer to tell the dream a second time and ask for the feelings at each point in the dream. When is the dreamer angry, sad, fearful, joyful, loving, hopeless, excited, aroused, or overwhelmed?

One of the things I listen for is the progression of feelings. Does the dream start out neutral and then turn sour or frightening? Do things begin pleasantly and then become chaotic or turn into disaster? And how is this like the dreamer's life at the time of the dream? Or does the dream begin in the middle of a problem situation and the dreamer then solves it on her own? Does she ask for assistance? Is she helpless and hiding? Does she run away? Does she defend herself, speak up, or scream to get the attention of others? All these details of the emotional state and action will be clues to the meanings of the dream for this dreamer. How a dreamer handles his dilemmas in his dream world will tell us how he is handling a problem (or most of his problems) in his waking life.

I look for the statements and words that have the most energy. Frequently, the tip-off is a curse word or some other emotionally charged term, especially when this is not a regular part of the person's speech pattern. A dreamer who ordinarily chooses his or her words with care but then describes a dream character as an *asshole* is conveying more than opinion. This strength of feeling may be key to getting to these feelings in waking life that may have been denied, repressed, or rejected as unacceptable.

What about dreams of people who are dead or no longer in our lives? Why do we dream about friends from high school or famous people we never met?

Once again, we look at both the object and subject levels. If the person is no longer in the dreamer's life or never has been—as in the case of a famous person—then we might look for a link to someone currently in the dreamer's life. Old events come up because there is some congruence, some similarity with the dreamer's current life situation and feelings. If I dream about having a fight with a childhood neighbor, I might ask myself how the feelings in the dream felt like something that happened in my life the day of the dream. Did I feel the same hostility, anxiety, or fear with someone at work? With someone I thought was a friend, but whose loyalty and friendship I now doubt? What's the connection to today?

While the dream may be the expression of a forgotten memory, it comes up now for several reasons. As we said in chapter 1, perhaps our present strength gives us the ability to deal with this old trouble. But the dream presents itself using these images and metaphors because the memory of this old trouble is of significance right now. As in waking life, we compare our present experience with old experiences that we have handled well or those that we have bungled. We use that experience as a way to deal with our existing dilemmas to find solutions to them. We practice our new behaviors in our dreams so we might act on them in the future.

·four·

Basic Dreamwork Techniques

WORKING ON YOUR DREAMS ALONE

Most of the techniques discussed in this chapter and the next can be used when working with your dreams alone. If you want to work with your dreams, I suggest that you begin by keeping a dream journal. The act of keeping a daily journal, even one not initially intended for the recording of dreams, will also facilitate remembering your dreams.

KEEPING A DREAM JOURNAL AND DIARY

For the last several years, I have followed the advice of Julia Cameron (1992), by making a journal entry every morning on waking. Though she recommends writing in longhand while you are still in bed and not fully awake, I choose to write at my computer. At this time, I write what I'm feeling, my thoughts and concerns, including the details of my activities of the previous day. I also record any dreams from the previous night. While I have a notebook at my bedside to write down a few phrases about my dreams, this isn't where I fully record the dreams. I do that when I do my journal entry at the computer. That's the time when I try to capture as many details and feelings as possible. Even if I don't have enough time to work with the dream to explore the layers of meanings, I try to record it all though I may not be able to list my associations.

When you write down your dream the first time, especially if you write in the middle of the night and intend to go back to sleep, your notes needn't be long or elaborate. Even a short entry will assist in opening the doorway to your unconscious and to the world of your dreams. A few phrases such as, "in school—no clothes—can't find classroom" will often be enough to bring a whole dream back to you. (These are very common dream themes. See chapter 9 for a more complete discussion of common dreams.) I repeatedly find when I begin writing down a fuzzy, broken dream that is barely remembered when I wake up, more and more details come into focus and I remember more parts of the dream as I write or talk my dream out. It is as if each piece is linked to another piece and I am drawing it into my conscious mind link by link.

Perhaps you've had the experience of remembering a fragment of a dream, often just the last piece before waking. As you proceed to tell it to someone, a bit more is remembered, perhaps the preceding dream scene. As you tell that one, another piece is available. Each dream memory is attached to the one before and we will often remember the dream in reverse order, recording backwards. When working with a dream, you can begin to examine the elements and scenes in any order. The final meanings will be available when you look at all the pieces together.

When keeping a dream journal, I strongly suggest you make some notes about what you did on the day of the dream, even if it's only a brief list of activities. Since dreams are about what is current in your life and what is on your mind at the time of the dream, your daily events, recorded along with your dreams, will help you to make connections between the two.

Let us suppose I have a dream about my sister. If I haven't seen her and she isn't on my mind at the time of the dream, then I need to explore why I am dreaming about her now. Looking back at the day of my dream, I might discover that I had lunch with my closest friend, the one I think of as a sister. Further, the interaction while we were together called up feelings that unconsciously reminded me of my sister, which may be positive or not. More likely, they will be an amalgam of emotions including rivalry, possessiveness, irritation, responsibility, affection, joyful sharing, fear of loss, intimate connection, family loyalty. This is my personal list, of course. The connections another person might make in similar circumstances or those I might make at another time will likely be different. What I need to see is how my personal concept of "sister" and all that is attached to it (very powerful feelings for me) is related to my present relationship with this friend and perhaps the other women in my life.

When we record our daily events along with our dream images and we see the two simultaneously, we can begin to make the connections to some of the levels of meaning in the dream. Always keep in mind that each dream is about what happened in your life in the previous twenty-four hours or so, and those issues that were most on your mind at that time. The dream will be comprehensive, including nearly all the important areas of your life in some literal and/or metaphoric way. Also, over time, certain symbols may emerge again and again.

Keeping a dream journal helps us to see the patterns in our symbols. Through journaling, we have the benefit of seeing dreams as part of a series and see the changes we make as they are expressed in our dreams. Journals help us to see how our problems are temporary. What seems unsolvable and the end of the world one day may seem humorous or unimportant a year later. Journals give us perspective, patience. They remind us that this, too, shall pass. They prevent us from taking ourselves too seriously—or not seriously enough. They remind us that we've made the same mistake before and it's time to make a change. For me, journal writing and dream-work are inseparable. Both keep me more honest with myself.

WHY WE MAY NOT WANT TO SHARE OUR DREAMS: PRIVACY, SECRETS

Many people express their concern about writing personal information in a diary or journal where it might be read by others. They point out that diaries have become a source of evidence in court cases and others have had their reputations sullied because of information disclosed in a diary that they assumed would never be made public. For them, a journal puts them at personal risk, perhaps legal and/or political risk as well.

On the other hand, there are those who assert that having secrets of any kind is a sign of illness or emotional instability and shame. The argument goes something like: Surely, if we fully accept ourselves as we are and we are living ethically and with integrity, then we should have nothing to hide from anyone.

While there is some truth to this, I believe that we have to set our own boundaries about what we want to disclose about ourselves to others. It is common today for people to go on television talk shows and reveal the most personal details of their families and their sexual proclivities, their past actions of immorality and violence. I doubt that this kind of disclosure makes these people any "healthier" than those in the population who share themselves with a few chosen, trusted individuals in a measured way that is comfortable and takes into account the consequences of disclosure. I believe that a need for privacy and secrets exists at times and only the holder of the secret should decide what to expose and whom to expose it to. I am not in favor of "outing" others against their will.

However, a journal or diary should be a place where you can be yourself without censoring the content or the language, where you can express yourself without fear of the consequences to yourself or of hurting those you write about. It should be a place where you can say all the terrible things you would never say in front of others and might even have a hard time saying to yourself. These dark moments may be only that and are not a statement of your overall character or the way you treat people. Mean or perverse thoughts (subjective terms at best) are not the same as deeds and do not carry the same power in the world. Occasionally venting these emotions and desires is one way to release them from having a hold on you. When you release them safely, you can prevent your turning them into behaviors that you might regret or that might have negative consequences on your life.

Your journal, therefore, should be private. You should be able to write in it without worry that someone will read it without your permission. If you live alone, it's pretty easy to keep your personal materials private. However, if you live with others, it's important to feel secure that the privacy of your journal will be respected. If you have any doubts, then you should find a place to keep it where you will feel secure that it won't be read. Some people use the trunk of their car or a combination safe in the house. A computer journal offers the possibility of keeping the journal files on floppy disk (rather than a hard drive) and storing these in a safe place away from snooping eyes. One woman used a safe deposit box at the bank, and she went there to write in one of the private rooms. It seems to me that if someone feels the need to go to these extremes to ensure privacy, it indicates a serious problem in her relationship that needs to be addressed. Of course, these problems would be uncovered in the person's dreams as well. Feeling that your privacy is threatened, in itself, can be an opportunity to work on issues of honesty, privacy, and trust in your relationships.

The important aspect of journal keeping is that you find a way to do it so that you can feel secure and free to write without censoring yourself.

DISADVANTAGES TO WORKING ALONE

While you will be able to do some valuable dreamwork while working on your own, you will most certainly miss many of the potential insights. Because we all have our blind spots, it is often hard to hear the glaringly clear metaphors in our own dreams. When we hear another's dream, we wonder how the dreamer could miss what the dream is saying because the metaphor is so obvious to us. That is why I recommend working in groups or at least with a dream partner. (See chapter 6 for dreamwork in groups.)

Still, solitary dreamwork is better than no dreamwork at all. Just the act of recording the dream seems to offer an opening to possible meanings. Many people find that writing down their dreams provides some relief from the dream's sometimes distressing images. Once in the light of day, the demons and monsters of dreams begin to lose their power. Fear evolves into curiosity. By trying to understand the meaning of these bizarre images, we begin to hear our poetry and creativity.

LITERAL MEANINGS FIRST

The first level of meaning is often a literal one. No matter what the content of the dream, it's a good idea to see how the image and story of your dream might have some truth exactly as they appear.

For example, if you dream of your teeth falling out, you might want to check your teeth. Perhaps the dream is an early warning of a problem or a crown is coming loose. You might taste an abscess at a less-than-conscious level before you have other symptoms. Any dreams with concrete images of our bodies or parts of our bodies should first be examined as diagnostic information, perhaps of some illness or a tendency toward acquiring some illness. The dream might be telling us our present lifestyle needs to be changed if we are to be healthy.

The next step is to look at how these images are metaphors for something in your life. What happened in the dream? Did you lose a tooth? How did you feel? What would a lost tooth mean to you? For one person, it might be the fear of loss of attractiveness. To another, it might call up fears of aging and being frail in some way. Perhaps there is something you can't sink your teeth into. Do you use an expression with the word tooth in it? Are you having to fight someone tooth and nail? I would ask the dreamer how not having teeth would feel. Is he worried about not being able to eat? Does she say she can't bite without teeth? If you can't chew, then you can't swallow. I want to know what the dreamer can't swallow in life. Or perhaps the feeling is one of having bitten off more than she can chew. If the teeth feel like they're crumbling, I wonder what might be crumbling or falling apart in the dreamer's life. Does this represent emotions crumbling?

It is usually the literal layer of meaning that frightens many people away from doing dreamwork. They are afraid a truth might be contained in the dream or worry the dream might be a prophecy of events to come. If I have a dream of a loved one being in a serious car accident, I would examine if there might be some truth to this possibility. Perhaps I rode as a passenger and noted, on some level just out of conscious awareness, a problem with her car. The problem might have been subtle, but I may have become aware of it through a feeling or peripheral thought in the middle of conversation. Maybe the steering seemed loose or the brakes made a squeak that wasn't yet conspicuous. I might have noticed a friend is driving less cautiously than usual or seems to have his mind on other things as he drives.

My observation might have faded from awareness as our normal conversation continued, but the memory remained at an unconscious level to rise again in my dream. If I have such a dream of someone having an accident, I will share that with the person. It doesn't mean he will really have an accident if I don't tell him. After all, nearly everyone has a car accident at some point. Since I don't know whether people are able to see into the future in some yet-unknown way, I feel I have a responsibility to share this information with the person.

METAPHORICAL MEANINGS OF DREAMS

Most dreams have the richness of meanings contained at the metaphorical level. By not examining the metaphorical layer, people miss the layers of other possible meanings. They think they dreamed about their teeth because they went to the dentist that day or because they have a toothache. These experiences may be why they had the image of teeth, but there is more meaning in dreams than just a rehash of the day's events. In dreams, we are often turning events over in our minds, making sense of them in ways we didn't in waking life.

To get to the metaphorical layer, it is helpful to look at exactly how the events happen in the dream and the words used to describe them. The image of spitting out teeth whole is quite different from feeling them crumbling or rotting out in your mouth. As you read about these mental pictures, you are probably reacting emotionally. These reactions are clues to the meaning of the dream for you if this were your dream. What memories are associated with teeth for you and what emotions are attached to those memories? Once again, these personal reflections reveal the meaning of the dream in a way no dictionary can. This is also why I cannot answer the question "I had a dream about my teeth. What does that mean?" The dreamer has to say a lot more and then he will come to his own conclusion about what meanings his dream about teeth might hold for him. For me, a dream about teeth might mean something entirely different. I have several crowns, and my tooth dream might get me to issues of my own grandiosity revealed by the word *crown*. Dentures might bring up issues of being false in some way.

LANGUAGE AND PLAYS ON WORDS

To investigate the metaphorical layers of meaning, I ask the dreamer about her use of language. I look for figures of speech using the language of the dream, as with the tooth dream. A friend of mine often uses the expressions *plugged in* and *connected*. In her dreams, electrical outlets and sockets appear, making a picture of this phrase. She looks where the wires go, wondering if they are connected to anything, and this reflects how she evaluates other people. Are they connected or not?

Many of the expressions we use are already on a metaphorical level. We talk about people crapping all over us, biting off our heads, taking shots at us. We talk about having ants in our pants, say we're jumping out of our skins, wish we could hide in a hole or have the ground swallow us up. We say we're doing so well we're flying. We even talk about pleasure and ecstasy using the language of death: "It was so wonderful, I could have died" or "It's to die for."

We use these terms without meaning them literally, but in our dreams we turn them into literal images. When we tell the dream, we are so focused on the pictures and emotions of the dream that we are often unable to hear the common metaphors of everyday language. Writing descriptions of our dreams and reading them aloud helps us hear these expressions.

In a dream group, because the dreamer is intent on telling the dream, explaining the specific details, and trying to tell them clearly, he doesn't hear the metaphor in the dream about what his boss is giving him. He sees the image of being handed a box of feces, has a clear picture of what they look and smell like, and is embarrassed and conceivably disgusted at having to describe it to others. The group, unattached to the emotional content and removed from the images, immediately hears the metaphor and breaks into laughter. "So who's giving you shit?" they ask. Or "Who is crapping on you?" Or maybe the dreamer feels he's been handed a shitty job to do. The meaning will become clear to the dreamer at the moment he makes the connection.

As I listen to a dream, I am listening on several different levels. I am paying attention to possible plays on language that might be puns or clichés or slang words. I pay attention to how the person speaks and the expressions she uses. Each of us has our own peculiarities of language and usage and syntax; these will be reflected in our dreams. For an older woman who complained of dreams of being chased, I wrote out the word *chaste* for her. Her expression showed the impact of recognition.

A frequent example of plays on words can be seen in dreams about driving a car or other vehicle. If you feel as if you've been relegated to the backseat in a particular circumstance of your life, that's where you're likely to be in your dream. If a dreamer is a passenger in her own car and someone else is driving, I ask her how she is no longer in the driver's seat—in her life. We make a figure of speech a pictorial, literal image in a dream.

ASSOCIATIONS TO DREAM ELEMENTS

Once a dream is told, I ask the dreamer to talk about the individual dream elements. As in Freudian dreamwork, the dreamer is asked to relax some conscious controls and be given an opportunity to associate to the various elements and say what comes to mind. A bicycle in a dream recalls an accident the dreamer had when riding a bike at eight—just after the death of his mother. A fringed, antique lamp calls up a memory of the antique store the dreamer's aunt owned. *Each dream element opens the door to the personal world of the dreamer in a way that no dream dictionary can.* The dreamer's associations to a particular dream element will help unmask the meaning of the symbol in the dream as well as the meaning (or meanings) the entire dream holds for the dreamer.

FEELINGS IN DREAMS—THE KEY TO MEANING

Listening to someone tell a dream, I try to be present to the speaker more than just intellectually. I try to hear what the person is feeling as she tells her dream and the feelings she had during the dream. I watch for changes in the person's emotions in the course of telling the dream. Does she sound fearful? Is she holding back tears? Does she express embarrassment or disgust? Sometimes a dreamer will say an image or event was horrible or obscene but be smiling and laughing at the same time. This mismatch between content and feelings is a signal to me that there is something in this dream that the dreamer hasn't faced with honest feelings.

The whole dream presents an emotional state or sequence of states (e.g., curiosity to confusion to fear to terror) that helps reveal the meaning of the dream. The overall emotional state is extremely important to help the dreamer make the connection between his dream and his waking life. If the dreamer doesn't say what his feelings were at the time of the dream, I will ask him to tell the dream again, this time identifying the predominant feeling for each piece of the dream.

Just as important, I am attentive to my own emotional reactions as I listen. Sometimes my own reactions will help me in the questions I'll ask. If the images presented make me anxious or give me a feeling of dread, I might ask the dreamer whether she also has these feelings, knowing I might only be projecting my own feelings onto the dreamer. I watch to see how what I reveal about my own feelings affects the dreamer. But the dreamer is the final authority on what the dream means to her. More than once, a dream that sounded like a nightmare to me and other members of the group didn't feel like a nightmare to the dreamer.

For some people, talking about and expressing feelings is a new experience. At the beginning of dreamwork, they might not understand what I'm looking for. I ask, "How did you feel when you walked up to the house in your dream?" Instead of answering this question, the dreamer might say, "It was a big house. I never saw it before." This is good information for further work on the dream, but he didn't answer the question. I ask again how he felt. If I still don't get an answer, I might try asking in a more direct way. "How did you feel? Were you afraid? Curious? Happy?"

In general, I prefer not to be this directive, but it helps people who are not used to tuning in to their feelings. I'll make these possible suggestions across a range of feelings rather than saying only one or two. I know some of the emotions I suggest will be off base so the dreamer can correctly identify his own feelings. "Oh, no. I wasn't happy. I was terrified!" Sometimes, this exploration is so foreign for the beginning dreamer, we just have to wait for more dreamwork for him to be aware of how he feels. Other members of the group can help teach about this aspect of self-awareness when they talk about what their own feelings were while listening to the dream, or how they might feel if this dream had been theirs.

When we identify the predominant feelings in the dream, I ask the dreamer what happened the day before the dream that made him feel like this. Frequently, that one question will be enough to give the dreamer his first *aha* with this dream, his first connection with one of the meanings in the dream.

In one man's dream, he saw himself at a gathering of people and felt afraid, as if there were an evil force in the room. He wanted to run away, but felt he had to stay because his wife and children were there. When I asked him what had happened the day before, he remembered being at a meeting at work. It was easy to identify what he felt was the evil force. The company was restructuring, and his job was going to be redefined. He felt threatened and wanted to leave the meeting as well as the job, but knew he couldn't do either because of his responsibilities to his wife and children. This was an immediate connection to one layer of meaning in the dream based on the feelings alone.

DESCRIPTIONS OF DREAM ANIMALS, PLACES, THINGS, PEOPLE, EVENTS

When I ask for a description, I try to come to the image as if it were something I had never heard of before. This is difficult because I have my own thoughts and ideas about elephants, Ferris wheels, singles' dances, or whatever comes up in the person's dream. I want the dreamer's description because, like feelings, this will help the dreamer connect with the meaning of the dream.

The description a person gives to a particular element of the dream will be unique to the dreamer. When someone dreams about a lion, rather than thinking about lions in my own way, I want to hear how the dreamer thinks of lions in general and this particular lion in this dream. If the dreamer describes the lion as having big teeth and claws, a bloody mouth and a powerful body, that conveys a tone of danger and threat. A description of a lion as a kingly, endangered, beautiful animal of power, majesty, and grace presents a different point of view. Is the dreamer running from the lion or is he talking to it? All these descriptions lead to what personal meaning a lion has for the dreamer in this singular dream.

Gayle Delaney (1991) suggests we say to the dreamer, "I'm not from this planet. What's a lion? What is a lion like?" I find that using this technique helps me as the leader to let go of my own meanings attached to an image. This allows the dreamer to capture the special qualities of meaning that made him choose this symbol in his dream. The characteristics on which the dreamer focuses will help us see why this image appears in the dream. When I ask the question, "What's a lion?" in a group setting, I ask the other participants to refrain from blurting out what comes to mind before the dreamer has had an opportunity to identify his own description. The first few adjectives the dreamer chooses will be additional keys to unlocking the dream's meaning.

Perhaps because I conduct much of my work in Florida, the image of alligators shows up quite often in dreams. I am always awed by the first few words people might use to describe an alligator. One woman said it was "a big, dangerous animal with big teeth. When it bites down on you, it comes down with a lot of pressure." Another woman said the alligator in her dream was cute, up on its hind legs, more like a cartoon character, and was looking her in the eye. A third woman described an alligator as primitive, horny, low, and evil. It is interesting that in all three cases, these were women who recognized these alligators as the men in their life *as well as pictures of themselves.* I wouldn't make a leap to "alligators equals men" in women's dreams. However, the difference in the descriptions is striking. None of them are the first words that come to my mind for alligators. Each one reveals something unique and personal in the way they think of alligators and the person the alligator represents. In each case, the woman could also see in what way this description was a part of her also.

Similarly, I listen to descriptions of dream characters to hear what the tone and attitude of the dreamer is. This applies whether the person in the dream is someone known to the dreamer in his personal life, a famous person living or dead, or an unknown stranger. What is this person like?

The temptation of group members, including me, is to think of our own thoughts and feelings about a person, especially if it's someone we know such as another member of the group or a celebrity. Each of us comes to the idea of a person or a figure (mother, father, teacher) with our own concepts and experiences. One person might emphasize authority, another nurturing and tenderness, another mentoring. All this will be interesting for further exploration of the dream, but first we want to hear the dreamer's description without influence or contamination by the more confident and persuasive members of the group. For the first levels of exploration, it is the dreamer's words that count and will lead to understanding the dream's meanings.

IMAGE AS A METAPHOR OF THE BODY

When we dream of structures, vehicles, landscapes, or other three-dimensional images, it is sometimes helpful to look at these as possible representations of the body. One man told a dream in which he came out to his parked car and found that it had been damaged on the right side. In working with this on several levels, one could be seen as a metaphor of his body. He did, in fact, have some discomfort on the right side of his body, which he attributed to a muscle strain the day before. Since he'd received this injury while helping a friend move, he thought that finding the damage on his car was similar to finding the injury on his body the next day. In a way, he felt as if he'd been crashed into by this friend. (This had other metaphorical meanings in terms of this relationship.)

Similarly, finding yourself in a cave or other dark surrounding might represent a part of the body. We ask the dreamer how she felt and what she found in the cave. This line of questioning might lead us to consider some insidious illness of which the dreamer has an awareness only unconsciously. A woman dreaming of a moldy cave or purse might be aware of an illness in her uterus or her feelings about entering menopause. If the former interpretation resonates with her, she might want to investigate this possibility with a physician. On another level, the dream might be a representation of how she feels about her reproductive and sexual organs. Having been celibate for a long time, one woman described her genitals as dried out and dead. For her, seeing images in a dream of dried and neglected flowers might be a metaphor of her sexual organs.

Dreams of houses (also discussed in chapter 9) might be about the body or the dreamer's assessment of his body. Dreams of houses crumbling or falling down, leaky roofs, or cracked foundations are common among elderly people. As they begin to have problems with arthritis, joint stiffness, and broken bones, they are likely to represent these in their dreams as old buildings or houses in disrepair.

IMAGE AS A METAPHOR OF THE MIND

In a similar manner, we use structures as a metaphor of the mind or the emotions. We might ask the dreamers above how they feel they are falling apart, a figure of speech that we literalize in our dreams to say we feel we are emotionally unstable. An image of glass shattering might be a way to say we feel shattered. If we feel we are in a rut, we may find ourselves in a gully or ditch in our dreams. Our language has many terms for mental illness that capture structural imagery such as saying that you are having a breakdown. If your car breaks down in the dream, that might be how you feel about yourself. This can be an important warning to get a checkup, slow down, rest, or take better care of yourself.

Other images that might capture the figures of speech for mental problems or lapses are: having a screw loose, being out of your tree. If you say you've gone over the edge or are about to take the plunge, these could show up as pictures in our dreams. We might say someone is cuckoo, daffy, dotty, nutty, buggy, or twisted. Terms such as loon, nut, and fruitcake are used to indicate our suspicion that someone isn't in her right mind. We might say she's gone off her rocker or is off the beam. Any one of these figures of speech can be turned into visual illustrations in our dreams to represent these feeling of mental and emotional deficiency in ourselves and others. Dreaming of butterflies crowded into a small space on the night before a presentation could be a literal view of the nervous agitation we feel before a performance. Don't we say we have butterflies in our stomachs?

One dreamer didn't want to go down in the basement. She knew there had been a flood down there and the water was dirty and stagnant. Small, disgusting animals inhabited the space and the toilets had overflowed. This was a woman who had just begun to do inner work and she didn't like some of what she was learning about herself. In the dream, she knew she had to clean up this mess though she didn't want to do it. She made the decision she would do what she had to do, even if she had to get some help—her therapist. But she couldn't leave this mess. Later in the dream, however, the building turned into a lighthouse with a bright, shining beam of light for others to use to find their way. This second image balanced the negative view of herself since she could also see herself as a leader and a shining light to others. In her work as a teacher, this was a positive and realistic view of herself, though perhaps a bit self-inflated in the dream.

DREAM ELEMENTS AND PEOPLE: ARE THEY WHAT THEY APPEAR TO BE OR PARTS OF THE DREAMER? ARE THEY THEMSELVES OR SUBPERSONALITIES OF THE DREAMER?

One way to work with dreams is to look at each element (person, animal, place, object, structure, action, etc.) as a part of the dreamer as we did above. Fritz Perls, in defining Gestalt Therapy, said that everything in a dream is the dreamer, with each element representing some unknown or denied aspect of the dreamer's psyche or personality. This view is helpful and is one technique for exploring a dream's meaning. If your dream is about chaos or depicts a messy view, I might ask you if you feel you are in a chaotic situation or if your life is a mess.

Certainly, we deny what we think of as the darker aspects of ourselves by projecting them onto other things, people, situations. We see them as outside of ourselves rather than acknowledging that we have urges and desires we consider socially unacceptable or not in keeping with the image we hold of ourselves.

When I speak publicly, a question that nearly always comes up is whether the people in our dreams are aspects of our own personalities. Might they instead be who they appear to be? If I dream about my mother, is this a statement about my mother (or a mother-figure in my life now) or is it about the part of me that's like my mother? How do I know which one is right?

The answer is that they are both right, but at different layers of meaning in the dream. There isn't any one correct interpretation of a dream. The dreamer will find many layers of meaning, and some of those might even depict opposite points of view. This is not a contradiction in interpretations, but rather a way the dream captures our inner conflicts. Likewise, people in our dreams can be *both* aspects of ourselves and tell us something about them or our evaluation of them separate from us.

For example, if you dream about your husband or wife, you can work with this dream on several levels. First, I would suggest you look at how you feel about this person in the dream, what the person's behavior is, and how you respond. Is the behavior in the dream similar to this person's behavior in waking life? If the person does something you think he or she would never do in waking life, perhaps your dreaming self is trying to show you an aspect of this person you haven't seen before or refuse to look at consciously. Is the behavior an exaggeration of something that happened the day before but you overlooked because it was more comfortable to do so? We could look at how this image of your husband or wife is a more accurate representation. Perhaps it comes to balance your waking view as so wonderful or so terrible. A dream about a mate cheating or lying might be a message from our unconscious to let us know that we have suspicions that we are blocking out of our waking awareness. Having such a dream doesn't mean he or she is cheating, but it may mean we don't want to consciously consider this possibility. We may be ignoring or trying to ignore changes in him that are unmistakable signs of cheating. Though people say the husband or wife is the last to know, they may have known—at least unconsciously—for a long time, but didn't want to see the truth.

After exploring this layer of meaning, we might then ask if this representation of your mate is a way of seeing yourself more clearly. That is, whatever you are blaming and accusing the other person of in your dream (or in waking life) is something you are guilty of, but have refused to own as yours. Perhaps you, the dreamer, are the cheater. If you have recently found yourself strongly attracted to someone other than your mate, you might be having an inner struggle that you haven't yet allowed to come to consciousness. This can be expressed by putting the behavior and the feelings onto someone else. You might dream your spouse or best friend is having an affair, but that might be a projection of your own desires onto others.

Please note: In the previous paragraphs, I'm using the societal norms of fidelity and monogamy. Certainly, if you live a more open lifestyle that includes responsible nonmonogamy or a loving network of friends and multiple mates, then the term *cheat* may have more to do with other kinds of dishonesty than clandestine sexual encounters. Your values and ethics as well as your use of language will be reflected in your dreams, especially when they differ from the norms of your cultural group.

Characters in dreams may be looked at as individual subpersonalities of the dreamer. The snobby woman or the mean boss in my dream might actually be a look at myself in a way that I am unable to see myself in waking life. Sometimes this facet of your personality is wonderful, creative, and generous. You might see yourself as a philanthropist, a dancer, a painter, and this can lead you to express these neglected but positive aspects of yourself.

YOUR CORE ISSUES

Remember that we always dream about what is most on our minds. If I have anxiety about my roof leaking, the burglaries in my neighborhood, or feeling neglected by my family, then those will be the images and feelings I dream about. But any one of these dreams may have more than one layer of meaning beyond the first and obvious layer. Beyond these everyday and immediate concerns, we will symbolize what I consider to be core issues. Sometimes, these are problems and questions that seem to burden us all our lives, as if contained in them is our life task or our mission statement for being on the planet. For one person, it might be dealing with authority figures, for another, living responsibly and being accountable for his actions. Some people spend most of their lives searching for spiritual answers or for their proper life's work. Some spend many years coming to terms with trauma, sexual guilt, or handling their finances. These, too, will be evidenced in their dreams. At one level, the dream may be current and reflect the day's concerns, but looked at more globally, we see the core issues of the individual reflected in many if not all of his dreams.

You might want to investigate what your core issues are since they are what is most important to you, whether you are aware of them or not. Frequently, they will appear in your dreams by way of repeated symbols and recurrent dreams and themes. One of my core issues has been how forces outside of me (religions, government, society, parents, authority figures, experts, lovers) have tried to influence me or impose their definition of what I should be. This theme showed up consistently in my thoughts and dreams as well as when I was writing fiction.

YOUR PERSONAL DREAM DICTIONARY

Since we use the same symbols repeatedly even after we know what they are, we can write our own personal dream dictionaries. I recommend doing this if you want to work with your dreams on a regular basis. The listing for DOG would be different in my personal dictionary than it would be for someone who is afraid of dogs. In fact, each of my dogs represents a subpersonality of mine: one is feminine, timid, and a true princess. She demands I open doors for her and barks for a cookie when I'm on the telephone. The other is fearless, an adventurer, and stubborn. She's the risktaker and is sometimes too trusting. When my dogs appear in my dreams and they change appearance or die, I know these aspects of myself are changing. I don't see these dreams as prophecies of the death of my dogs, but rather as statements about my current life situation. Dreamers with children or students will sometimes use them instead of dogs to represent parts of themselves.

PERSONAL USE OF MODES OF ORIENTATION
(KINESTHETIC, VISUAL, AUDITORY MODES)

Neuro-linguistic programming (NLP) demonstrates that people have individualized modes of relating to the world. Anthony Robbins (1986) breaks these down into submodalities. For example, a visual person will be attuned to light and dark, size, color, shading, focus, depth of view. His speech would use the metaphors of visual experience: to look at a concept, to determine whether something is shallow or deep. He verbalizes in visual language.

An individual who relies more on kinesthetic and sensory modalities will be aware of temperature, pressure, movement of the body, weight, and texture. Auditory people will rely heavily on hearing, being aware of sounds others might miss, as well as being conscious of tone, pitch, volume, rhythm. These are only partial lists, but we can readily observe how these waking modes of awareness will be reflected in dreams as well as our waking state. Though all of us have all the modes available to us and use our five senses, we are likely to rely on one of these more exclusively than the others. When someone describes a dream, we can hear the weight placed on one of these modalities. A particular dream might have more movement and sensation in it while another might be more visual. Dreams characterized as being extremely vivid and real often have all the modalities, thereby engaging several of the senses. Some dreamers will report taste and smell in their dreams, but these are less common than the other senses or modalities. Awareness of more sensory information adds to making the dream seem real and ensures its being memorable—sometimes for many years afterward—just as these details add to our ability to remember events in waking life.

Knowing your own preferred orientations will help you when you work with your dreams. A kinesthetic person might use more grasping images and terminology while one who is more auditory will talk about what people say in her dreams, emphasizing dialogue more than what she is doing or how the scene appears visually with color, texture, lighting, or other visual descriptions predominating. We can notice these modalities in an individual's use of speech and metaphor. One might say any of the following to convey the same meaning:

Do you hear what I'm saying? (auditory)
Can you grasp what I mean? (kinesthetic)
Do you see it the way I do? (visual)

(For more information on Neuro-linguistic Programming, see books by Richard Bandler.)

PERSONAL IMAGERY

Clearly, each person develops a preferred way of imaging events and feelings. Rather than assuming our dream symbols and images are disguises, we can look upon them as the best possible representation we have created to express something to ourselves. They are chosen to reveal a truth rather than to confuse or mystify. The example I gave earlier of each of my dogs representing sub-personalities is a perfect illustration of how we rely on our own personal imagery. If I were using the dogs as a symbol to disguise, then I would surely change the symbol once I figured out what it was. On the contrary, my little white poodle continues to represent the princess side of me. No other symbol could capture it more vividly or concisely. Because of my strong affection and attachment to my dogs, dreams about them and what happens to them get my attention in a way that few other images can.

PAST EVENTS/EXPERIENCES AS PERSONAL METAPHORS

Sometimes, a past event becomes a personal metaphor for the dreamer. Many years ago, I quit a job where I had been working for several years. Every once in a while, I will have the following dream or one of a similar variation:

> I am working in a hospital laboratory again and I have been given a task to do with no explanation. The person who tells me what to do won't explain it and is annoyed when I ask questions. She says I should know what to do because I used to work there. When I protest that I haven't worked there for years, she walks away, annoyed

with my bothering her. I feel overwhelmed. I'm afraid I will make a mistake. I know there is more work than I can possibly finish in the time allotted and I am panicked. Then I realize that I've quit this job before. "I quit!" I say. "I don't have to work here!" And I then wake up.

At first, I thought I still harbored bad feelings about this job. Certainly, that's true in part, but the more important question that I ask myself as I ask any dreamer, "Why did you have this dream now? What is going on in your life that feels the way that job used to feel? And what do you want to quit now?" For me, this dream has come up when I've been struggling in a personal relationship, when I've turned a recreational activity into a stressful job, when I've been trying to do the impossible.

This dream is a good example of how we use symbols and metaphors in a personal way. Quitting this job has become a personal metaphor for my needing to quit other things or at least feeling as if I want to. At various times, this symbol has represented my yoga classes, a relationship, and even my emotional state on a vacation when I felt as if I was doing too much. The dream comes when I am stressed out or feeling unappreciated. It's a warning dream for me and is now part of my personal dream dictionary. My unconscious is saying, "Oh, this feeling is familiar. It's like when you worked at the hospital. You know what you did then? You can do it again. Time to check out for a while."

CAUTION: EACH DREAM IS ONLY A SNAPSHOT!

Because the dream is only a snapshot of the day's feelings and impressions, I discourage dramatic action based on a single dream. Certainly, there are days when you want a divorce or you hate your job, but that doesn't mean the feeling is the entire picture or this is what you should do. We are often ambivalent about the issues of most concern to us. We simultaneously love and hate many things in our lives, especially those that are most important, such as our mates, children, jobs, homes. The dream may give us the flip side of our conscious feelings, but it doesn't mean we should take the opposite extreme in our behavior. Rather, the dream is a reminder to stay balanced and honest with ourselves. One day I hate my house and I want to move; tomorrow I find myself enjoying this space and grateful I live here. My dreams of each night will reflect the feeling of the previous day and may not give the full story of my feelings or what I should do in any particular circumstance. Each dream is a piece of the larger puzzle of our lives.

DREAMS IN A SERIES

When you do dreamwork regularly through dream diaries or in a dream group, you will be able to see the dreams as a series that have a natural progression reflecting your growth and improved understanding. You will see that certain dreams appear at certain times in your life. A series of dreams will show you the path you are on and might indicate some changes you want to make. Or the dreams might remind you of your progress.

DREAMS OF ONE EVENING

In a similar vein, dreams collected from the same night are usually all on the same subject or related in a significant way. Each dream may appear to be different and use dissimilar images and metaphors, but each one is only an equivalent means of telling the same story. When working with several dreams from a single evening, I suggest working with each one individually first, and then seeing what connections can be made between them. They may be various ways of expressing the same problem or different ways of coping with an issue. One dream may help explain the meaning(s) of another.

LONG DREAMS

Many people have long, involved dreams with many, many details, shifts of scenes, characters, and story lines. The task of recording these dreams becomes daunting and cumbersome. People with this dreaming pattern will often give up working with their dreams because the task is so time-consuming and overwhelming. In this case, I suggest taking one of the more vivid and emotional scenes in the dream and focusing on that as if it were the whole dream. As with having too many dreams to record (see chapter 2), working with one piece in detail will offer helpful information. Often the other scenes and details are repeats of this same message, as we saw in dreams of the same evening.

DREAM FRAGMENTS

Dream fragments can be loaded with information. Think of them as perfect little poems and explore every word. One dreamer complained she only had skinny, ordinary, short dreams.

> I am at a buffet table. I take a very small bowl of food because I want to be sure that others will have enough.

On looking at the content, we discovered this dreamer said a lot with an economy of words—just as she did when she wrote poetry in waking life. She was not feasting at life's banquet because she was more concerned about the needs of others, thereby neglecting her own needs. The dream and the discussion that followed told her that she needed to set time aside for herself for daily writing.

Whether dreams are complex, simple, or scary, they can be worked with in a variety of ways to reveal their range of levels of information.

·five·

Additional and Advanced
Dreamwork Techniques

OFTEN, WHEN WORKING WITH DREAMS, WE
get stuck and find it difficult to uncover the meanings. At other
times, we feel the dream suggests further exploration. In this
chapter, we'll look at additional techniques for working with
dreams.

PREPARATION FOR SPECIAL TECHNIQUES:
MEDITATION OR RELAXATION

Before trying these methods, I suggest you begin with a short
relaxation or meditation to bring yourself to a more centered state.
It is important to be prepared in the sense of opening up to the
world of dreams and the unconscious. Begin by sitting quietly and
doing some deep breathing, being fully aware of the sensations in
your body, letting the usual chatter of your thoughts quiet down.
The constant mind babble we are all familiar with can drown out
the voices of our Higher Self and our unconscious, which is the
source of our dreams and creativity. (See the Appendices, p. 193,

for more detailed descriptions of relaxation and meditation styles for working with dreams.) Even a two- or three-minute relaxation can be helpful in opening up to the unconscious. The more often you relax and breathe, the more quickly you'll be able to reach this open state.

DREAM INCUBATION

It is possible to request a dream on a particular subject or about a particular person. Some people refer to this as programming or incubating their dreams.

Perhaps you'd like a solution to a problem that has been plaguing you or you're undecided about a course of action. A relationship may feel problematic and in need of a new approach or a strategy for making peace.

To incubate a dream, here are some steps you might want to follow:

1. Focus on the location where this dream might take place to bring you the answer you seek. If I wanted some clarity on my relationship with my parents, I'd use the setting of my childhood home since that's where my dream would most likely take place.

2. If you want information about someone or the relationship you have with this person, think about him/her as vividly as you can. Recall the sound and pitch of his/her voice.

3. Vividly imagine this person in your mind, or gaze at a photo if you have one.

4. If you are trying to solve a problem, write out the problem as you see it with a list of important facts that might impact on the solution.

5. Capture the feelings you are already aware of on the subject. For example: fear, anger, confusion, or hope. Let these feelings be a part of you without trying to change them or stifle them because they give you discomfort or guilt. Acknowledge the feelings as real without judging them.

6. Formulate a question or request in the simplest language you can, remembering that the unconscious mind is literal as well as metaphorical. Be as specific as possible. For example: Show me a new way to understand Carla. Or . . . Who am I when I'm with Carla? Recite this phrase to yourself throughout the day.

7. Write this question in your dream journal before going to sleep.

8. When you wake up, record whatever you remember of a dream, even if your dream appears nonsensical. If the dream appears to be about another subject, write it down anyway.

9. No matter what you dream, review it in terms of your request. Most probably, it will be an answer in metaphor or symbol to the question you asked. Though I might dream about my mother or grandmother, the dream is probably telling me something NEW AND HELPFUL about Carla, if that's what I've asked for.

10. Keep in mind that you can use this information only to change yourself, not others.

11. Remember that you will always get an honest answer, even if it's not the answer you wanted.

Some people become very proficient at programming their dreams. Even without such elaborate preparation, simply holding your question in mind as your last thought at bedtime might be enough to get an answer to a question.

Don't give up. Keep trying and expect an answer. You will be amazed at the wisdom you have within you.

PROBLEM SOLVING AND DECISION MAKING

Many, many important breakthroughs for scientists and artists have come through dreams. In some cases, they deliberately put the matter aside and went to bed with the question still lurking below the surface. When they awoke, they had a certainty of their solution, which they confirmed with further exploration or experimentation based on what their dreams revealed. Elias Howe's solution to making the sewing machine work, Kekule's concept of the structure of benzene as a ring, Beethoven, Mozart, Kipling, Coleridge, and Longfellow all credit some of their best work to have come in the dream state (Harman and Rheingold, 1984).

Once again, always assume the dream you receive is an answer to the question you asked. Because dreams are layered with meanings, at first your dream may appear to be about another concern in your life. This does not mean it wasn't an answer to the question you asked. It probably is both an answer to your question and a statement about other areas of your life. Consider the dream to be a metaphorical answer to your question.

Examples of problems or decisions you might want to use your dreams to help you with can be whether or not to continue in a new relationship, whether to change jobs, or simply asking your Higher Self how you're doing these days. Since dreams can sometimes give you indications of the health of your body, asking a health question can sometimes be helpful.

One dreamer asked whether a decision he was making was correct. When he dreamed he was pulling stones out of his ears, he had to consider whether the dream was telling him that he had rocks in his head to be taking this course of action. But there was also a literal layer to be considered since he had had some problems with his hearing. He could also ask himself what he was closed off to hearing by having the sound barrier of stones in his head.

Choose some current problem or dilemma in your life now. Maybe you'd like to know what to do in a relationship or how to take the next step in your personal growth. If you could ask a very wise person who would guarantee you an accurate answer, what question would you ask? Ask that question when you go to bed tonight and put it in writing in your dream journal. Expect an answer and record the dream you have. Work this dream with the expectation that the dream you had was an answer to your question.

DIALOGUING WITH DREAM OBJECTS, CHARACTERS, OR ANIMALS

Frequently, a character or animal will show up in a dream and the dreamer will have no idea why or what the significance might be. One way to work with these entities, whether they are living or dead, human or animal, is to create a dialogue or a conversation with this other being. Prepare yourself to hear whatever the message may be even if it isn't the one you'd like to hear.

You may tape record this dialogue or write it in your journal as you work or record it at the end of your dialogue. Don't expect to remember this without writing it down. Like dreams, any work with the unconscious and the insights received have a way of slipping away from us if we don't make an effort to hold on to the images and insights they bring. Make a habit of taking notes, especially when doing dreamwork with others. Write down your moments of *aha*, even if they came from working with someone else's dream.

After achieving a relaxed and receptive state, ask the animal what it wants or what message it has for you. Sit quietly and expect an answer. If nothing comes, you might imagine this creature more vividly by engaging your senses and asking it to fill in a sentence such as one of those below.

You are . . .

The time has come for . . .

Today is . . .

What you need to know is . . .

I have come to tell you . . .

Or you might let the character speak for itself with your voice, as Fritz Perls suggests. Be this person/animal/thing for a little while and see what it has to say.

I am . . . and I have come to say . . .

I bring you this dream to tell you . . .

One woman dreamed she saw an object pass through a wall. When she let the wall speak, she wrote:

> I am a *stone wall.* My surface is hard and rough, but
> I am no obstacle for those who are of spirit, those with
> unselfish love. I am no obstacle though I appear to be an
> obstacle. I am illusion when one sees beyond form. When
> clear of mind, when clear of soul, when a choice is made
> without any doubt, nothing is an obstacle, not even a
> stone wall.

The voice of the wall was completely unlike her own speech pattern and vocabulary. The message offered the encouragement she needed in taking the next step in her work. She had been holding back, feeling as if she were not up to the tasks ahead, but the dream image helped her see herself as more spiritually empowered and capable than she had thought of herself consciously.

When you are doing this work, don't censor the ideas or language that springs to mind. Nothing kills dreamwork more than trying to be proper or correct or follow the rules imposed on us by society or our conscience. If you worry about your dreams being unfeminist or how they show a racism you deny consciously, you will likely stifle what the dream has to offer. By doing this, you miss exactly what you need to learn from your dreams. You may be appalled at how opposed your dreams seem to be to your waking morality, philosophy, or political point of view. The images may be in sharp contrast to your values about yourself or beliefs in human and animal rights, but the dream is there for a good reason.

Dialogues with dream characters often reveal a wisdom we didn't know we had and can have ready access to if we allow ourselves to loosen up and hear the messages. The words used and the speech pattern may be very different from the dreamer's style. The dreamer in the example above was astonished at this lyrical prose and the emphasis on transformation as a spiritual process.

Many people express concern that they are making this up as they go along. That's fine. After all, you're the one who made up this character in your sleep, so "aking it up" when you are awake is not very different. If you can be present to whatever pops out of your mouth as this other character, then you may hear something new.

Because of the unpredictability of the outcome of a dialogue with a dream character, people are often fearful about doing this. What might they find out about themselves? What feelings might come up? It is helpful when you have these anxious thoughts to tell yourself that anything that happens is only temporary. You can be present to those uncomfortable emotions as a way to grow and understand yourself better. Getting in touch with our dark side of anger, rage, and violent impulses and making them conscious is the best method for keeping these emotions and urges in check. If we give these feelings a safe place for expression without endangering anyone, we remain fully in touch with all aspects of ourselves. Repressing them or pushing them out of awareness makes them stronger and subject to unconscious (mindless, impulsive) expression. Also, being open to whatever may arise will also give you an opportunity to see parts of yourself you will treasure. The Gestalt empty chair technique can be used to dialogue with dream characters as well (see Appendix O). And through these explorations, we can live more fully in the world with compassion and understanding for our fellow humans.

When you feel you are finished, ask your dream character if it has anything more to say. Then thank it for the help. (If this seems extraordinarily silly to you, remember you're simply expressing your cooperation with your unconscious processes.)

DRAWING, SCULPTING, PAINTING THE DREAM IMAGES AND FEELINGS

Sometimes drawing, painting, or sculpting our dream characters helps us discover who they are. We may better understand some detail as it reveals something we missed during the first telling of the dream. All this leads to further understanding and inner balance. Even when you are drawing abstract, unknown, and spontaneous designs or doodles, you are likely to discover you feel better afterward. You don't have to know why you feel better. If you've ever doodled on your notebook in class or at a meeting, you already have experience with this.

In dream workshops, when a dreamer is stuck on a particular dream image that seems resistant to revealing its symbolic value, I suggest doing a quick drawing. One woman had an image of single beds lined up side by side, with no space between them. I asked her to do a quick sketch for the group and then had her look at it herself. What does it look like? I asked. "Teeth," she said. And this brought a complete *aha*. She felt her romantic life (symbolized by the beds?) was hampered by the condition of her teeth and she wanted to have them corrected so they were lined up, straight, and white—like the beds in her dream. She felt the spaces between them were too wide.

Another woman said she was walking in a swamp of cypress knees. I wasn't sure if the other members of the group knew what this image might suggest, so I asked her to draw them. In her notebook, she drew the phallic-like objects, standing erect in the ground. "Penises!" everyone said at once. The dreamer said the swamp was menacing, dark, scary, and I asked her how those feelings related to this image. This brought a strong *aha* with tears and sobbing. She shared with the group her memory of being raped when she was in her twenties, an experience that still has an impact on her relationships with men. She had never told this to the group before, though she'd been a member for more than a year. The group provided the support and empathy she had needed for the thirty years since the event. Shortly afterward, the change in this woman was apparent: she was more animated and took up several new interests that she'd been afraid to explore before.

In both of these examples, it was important to see what the dream might be saying to them at this particular time. Why now? I want to know. What does the dream bring up for you that is relevant to your life in your present circumstances?

TRY THIS

For your next dream, in addition to writing it out, draw the images and see what the images suggest to you.

SOUND: CHANTING, TONING, GROANING

In many dreams, we are trying to shout or scream or say something. Often the dreamer has the feeling that no one is listening to his plea or that no one can hear him. These sounds and the words that come with them can have special meaning to the dreamer that remains out of awareness until the sounds are made.

If you were about to say something or shout out in the dream when you woke up, get back into the feelings of the dream through a short meditation and then make the sounds of the dream. See what this brings up for you and make a journal entry about it. This practice, which is called toning, can be part of your daily spiritual practice (Keyes, 1973).

DANCE AND MOVEMENT

Physical movement, or the attempt at it, is often seen in dreams. The dreamer may be pushing someone away or running or swaying. These actions can be brought into waking awareness through dance or movement. If you have such kinesthetic (body movement or sensations of physical orientation in space) experiences in your dreams, you might try acting them out with physical movement to see what hidden feelings or thoughts are behind these actions. See what comes up. Be present to these sensations with curiosity to see what you can learn about yourself. The movement or action might disclose something you missed in the language or story of the dream. These movements are also a way to access feelings that might be out of awareness, but close to consciousness.

UNSENT LETTERS

Many dreams bring up feelings of unfinished issues and experiences in the dreamer's life. This is especially true of relationships with family members, ex-spouses, or former lovers, who show up as characters in our dreams to haunt, torment, or pursue us. We often have unresolved or unaddressed feelings in our present relationships, too. One way to get to these feelings is to write a letter to the person, whether this person is living or not. The purpose is not to send the letter, but to express your feelings about him or her. Perhaps these are feelings we don't know how to express in a way that is acceptable to our own standards of proper behavior. If we believe we can't be angry at our parents or express our frustration with their mistakes, then we certainly cannot express our anger to them. More often, we haven't allowed ourselves to experience these emotions at all, and so they come out as our anger turned inward—through illness, depression, accidents.

Writing letters to the dream characters or unsent letters to those they represent can be liberating. We can say anything we want in these letters without fear of the consequences. By knowing we are NOT going to send the letters, we have complete freedom to use any language we care to, say anything we need to say. We cannot hurt someone by a letter we don't send, but we may feel better by having our say. In writing the letter, you don't have to consider the other's feelings or fear retaliation. As in a dream, you can take the lid off your raw emotions. Letting steam off in this safe way will free the energy we've wasted by keeping the anger or other emotion out of awareness.

Many people have a litany of grievances against their parents that they have been holding in for forty, fifty years. Those unexpressed emotions have been stuffed down with chemicals, food, sex, or dangerous lifestyles. Having a safe means for their expression often leaves the individual feeling released and unburdened by this relationship of the past. Susan Forward, in her book *Toxic Parents* (1989), recommends reading these letters at a gravestone, if necessary, as part of the process of healing the wounds of childhood.

I would like to add a word of caution here from my own beliefs about this work. My observation is that some people in the recovery movement seem to get stuck in this stage of inner work and healing. They have a certain anger, often justifiable, at a person's behavior and they go over and over a particular incident in their minds and in their discussions with others. They let the trauma define who they are and they become victims for the rest of their lives, never able to put the events of the past behind them. The purpose of the letter is to get closure, or at least to move in the direction of closure. We do not write the letters to open the wounds and wallow in them. Staying in this place gives more power to the problem rather than focusing on solutions and moving onward. Letter writing is a means of providing a container for these emotions but should not become a way of life in itself, bringing up bitter feelings over and over again. The letter should be one of the means of letting go.

TRY THIS

Choose someone (living or dead) who is no longer in your life, but with whom you still feel you have unfinished business. This may be a parent or an ex-spouse or some authority figure. Perhaps you have reason to feel this person should not be confronted in reality, but you may still harbor anger. Your adult wisdom and experience may tell you that you were unjustly treated in the past. Write that person a letter and don't hold anything back. Use the most powerful language you can, and don't worry about being polite. Get it all out. Then see how you feel.

Don't mail this letter.

RITUALS AND CEREMONIES

In conjunction with letter writing, I will usually suggest that the dreamer design a personal ritual for further closure. Sometimes, through dreamwork, a person will discover she has not completed grieving the death of a loved one. This is especially common in sudden, accidental deaths or suicides, or if the person did not attend a funeral for some reason. I suggest creating a ritual for saying good-bye to the deceased person and encourage the person to create the personal ritual that invokes the feelings and words needed for this person's feeling of closure. Some people want to have a ceremony in a favorite place they frequented with this absent person, such as a park where they once had a memorable picnic. Including an item they received as a gift from this person, they might light candles, say what was meaningful in the relationship, read their letter aloud, thank the person for being in their life, and say good-bye. Some people like to burn their message or even burn some small item that belonged to the lost loved one. The burning symbolizes transformation as well as farewell.

When designing a ritual, the dreamer is the person who should decide where and what should be done. While it's helpful to have a friend as witness, assistant, and support person, it's important that the person the ritual is for be the one designing the ritual. Friends are eager to give their ideas and become actively involved, but it's better if they are less involved and take more of a supportive role, without questioning the strategy of the ritual. The person's unconscious will offer up what is needed here.

You might also want to consider rituals for life's major transitions: your child's departure from home to live on her own, divorce, or the ending of a friendship. If the relationship has been close or meaningful, a ritual can help when people are separating for any reason. Many women create rituals for menopause or for turning fifty or sixty years old.

Rituals of confrontation and for expressing anger can be helpful where it is impossible or inappropriate to do this with the person present in reality. You might want to do this to deal with your feelings about an elderly or sick relative who might be too fragile to bear a real confrontation.

Robert Johnson's comments on ritual in *Owning Your Own Shadow* bear repeating:

> Remember, a symbolic or ceremonial experience is real and affects one as much as an actual event.
> The psyche is unaware of the difference between an outer act and an interior one. Our shadow qualities are lived out equally well—from the viewpoint of the Self— either way. Culture can only function if we live out the

unwanted elements symbolically. All healthy societies have a rich ceremonial life. Less healthy ones rely on unconscious expressions: war, violence, psychosomatic illness, neurotic suffering, and accidents are very low-grade ways of living out the shadow. Ceremony and ritual are a far more intelligent means of accomplishing the same thing. (Johnson, 1991)

William Carl Eichman agrees:

The actual process of healing and transforming the eruptions of the dark side can be very complicated. Because these dark complexes were written into the psyche during our childhood, reasoning with the "dark side" has almost no effect. On the other hand, rituals, purifactory regimes, healings, protective power objects, and special meditative and grounding exercises can all be of benefit when used in the right time and right place. The energy of the dark nature must be frequently released and expressed, and this should be done consciously, using art or ritual to prevent an excess flow of the psychic energy from harming family and friends. (quoted in Zweig & Abrams, 1991)

Some excellent rituals can be found in *Transformative Rituals*, by Gay and David Williamson (1994). These rituals are simple to arrange and can provide what is missing in getting closure on life issues. If you like the flavor of Native American ritual and ceremony, see *American Indian Ceremonies* by Medicine Hawk and Grey Cat (1990).

Performed with others participating, rituals are even more powerful. As with all the important events such as weddings, baptisms, graduations, having others present as witnesses and support lends more meaning and import to the ceremony.

TRY THIS

Think of someone who is no longer in your life for any reason, perhaps someone to whom you never had a chance to say good-bye. Design a simple ritual in memory of this person and the times you shared. Consider, as one possibility, returning to a favorite place you visited together. You might want to leave something there to say farewell—a feather, rock, shell, or leaf, maybe, with a short message attached. Feel that these memories are now officially in the past. You might choose to remind yourself you don't have to tell this story anymore to others or to yourself so that you are free to let go and move on.

LIST OF CHERISHED BELIEFS

Quite often, our dreams will call into question our most cherished beliefs about ourselves. Most of us are unaware of the beliefs and assumptions we carry with us about the world. It is a truism today that we create our own reality. On the one hand, if you believe people are not to be trusted, you are likely to find yourself among people who are untrustworthy, or perhaps you will bring out the parts of them that are not to be trusted. On the other hand, we carry our own idealized beliefs about ourselves, others, and the way the world "really" works. These sometimes need to be called into question because we are kidding ourselves, or conducting ourselves with an innocence or expectation that can be detrimental. Some commonly held cherished beliefs are:

I'm a good person.

I'm honest and reliable.

I can be trusted.

I'm considerate and caring of others.

My perception is accurate.

I am in control of my life and my destiny.

I don't judge others.

People can be trusted to be honest and tell the truth.
There is sense to this world and our place in it.
Goodness and truth will be rewarded.
Honesty is the best policy.
My job is secure.
I have a perfect relationship with my mother.
I can get along with everyone.
I have no enemies.

Our dreams will often challenge us on these beliefs, showing us how we are falling short of the idealized image we have of ourselves, pointing out our little (and not so little) dishonesties. They will also show us how we have over- or underestimated others.

And of course, the circumstances of our lives make us question our most cherished beliefs: faced with a serious illness, we realize we are not entirely in control of our lives; people we trust or depend upon may disappoint or betray us; the universe doesn't always seem to make sense. We frequently lose our innocence as we discover life is neither fair or predictable. Our dreams help us to acknowledge these upsets and to come to terms with them realistically when we have difficulty doing so consciously.

LISTS OF 100

Kathleen Adams in *Journal to the Self: Twenty-two Paths to Personal Growth* (1990) suggests making lists of a hundred things that you think or feel. I have used this method as another tool for doing dreamwork. Occasionally, the dreamer will feel stuck when working on a dream. The feelings the dream brings up are clear, but the reasons the emotions are present are not. I suggest focusing on the feeling and then making a list of 100 occasions that bring up this feeling. Use the breathing and centering exercises first and try to re-create the feeling in the dream as much as possible. If you are anxious or fearful in a dream, you might make a quick list of 100 circumstances that make you feel fearful or anxious. Number the lines on your pages from one to one hundred. Begin writing and don't stop until you're done, completing the list in one sitting. Afterward, you can review the entries for patterns, repeats, breakthroughs, and suggested actions for change. Perhaps you will discover that your anxiety or fear clusters around certain people or a particular environment such as your workplace. Making this list may help you reach the unconscious material the dream was probably bringing to consciousness with its strong emotions.

Some possibilities are:

100 things I'm afraid of

100 things that make me anxious

100 things I can't stand

100 things I'm good at

100 things that make my heart sing

100 things I want to do before I am XX years old

The process is meant to break through whatever is blocking the associations to the dream's feelings. A list of 100 of anything may seem like a lot to name, but Adams suggests you keep writing without thinking about what the correct answers are. It's okay to repeat, and you don't have to write in complete sentences or worry about the items making sense. In fact, when they become less sensible and more shocking or surprising, you will know you have touched upon unconscious material that you might only access through dreams otherwise.

Adams's book is an excellent companion for doing inner work.

TRY THIS

Write the numbers 1 to 100 on a piece of paper now and list the reasons why you believe doing dreamwork will be helpful to you. Have fun with this and don't worry about being silly or out-landish. That's when you get to the best stuff!

ASKING FOR A STATUS REPORT ON YOUR LIFE

Often, without asking or incubating a dream, we will get one that offers us a status report on how we are doing in our life. Perhaps we're beginning to feel we are backsliding or in a downward spiral, and our dreams will give us images and feelings, maybe even bodily sensations (of falling or sliding downward) to express this assessment. Flying dreams will often indicate how we feel we are soaring and feeling good about ourselves.

There will be times, however, when you'll want to ask for a status report. Perhaps you're aware of feeling stuck or unsatisfied and you wish you had a wise old guru to go to and ask for an evaluation or a report card. Of course, no one knows better how you're doing than you do. You can incubate a dream with this as your intention.

TRY THIS

Before going to bed, make sure your dream journal or note-book and pen are at your bedside within easy reach. Sitting up, phrase the question in your mind: *How am I doing?* or *What do I need to know about myself now that I'm ready to know?* Write the question in your journal and hold it in your mind as you turn off your light and fall asleep. Reminder: Assume that whatever you dream is an answer to your question or request.

INDUCING A DREAM TRANCE WHILE AWAKE

Some people who rarely remember dreams or would like to have dream material to work with *now* can induce a dream trance while awake. Choose from among the relaxation exercises in the Appendices, p. 193. Once you are in this state, continue to sit comfortably and wait for images to come to mind. If you have a favorite place you use for your relaxation or meditation, go there mentally and ask the question you would like an answer to, just as you would when incubating a dream or asking for a status report. Observe, as if watching a movie, the images, actions, characters, and animals that appear. You can work with this waking fantasy as you would a dream.

GETTING BACK INTO THE DREAM (AWAKE OR ASLEEP)—ALSO CALLED DREAM EXTENSION

Many people are disappointed when they wake up or are woken up in the middle of a dream. They want to know how the dream ends, or they were enjoying themselves more than they do when they are awake. When I teach, people often ask how they can get back to a dream. The other class members smile, recognizing the desire. Perhaps they were in the middle of a lovely erotic dream and they weren't done yet!

Whether or not the dream was sexual, you can reenter the dream state. Some people are able to do this by returning to the position they were in while sleeping, closing their eyes and staying with the image until the dream returns. If you find you can't do this, use the suggestions for entering a relaxed state and continue the dream.

TRY THIS

Choose a dream that was particularly interesting to you. Write about or draw the images of the dream and let them float around in your head before falling asleep or when entering a meditative state. Once again, observe and record, as if watching a movie, the images, actions, characters, and animals that appear and proceed to use these as you would any dreamwork material, whether or not these have surfaced in REM sleep or in a meditative state.

ACTIVE IMAGINATION

Similar to dream extension, active imagination allows the dreamer to continue to allow a dream to unfold or evolve without conscious control. Once again, the dreamer enters a relaxed or meditative state and then brings the focus to a particular dream element. In this relaxed state, unconscious material is likely to surface. By watching what happens to the dream image and the actions of this reverie, the dreamer can have additional information to work with for further knowledge about the self.

TRY THIS

Choose a dream image that you've had more than once. You might use a building or house of which you have a clear mental picture. Imagine you are seeing it again and observe how the image changes, grows, or becomes more or less distinct. How is this a metaphor for something in your life today?

REWRITING THE ENDING OF THE DREAM

Dreams with unhappy or unsatisfying endings do not have to remain so. Most people assume they have to go back to sleep and reenter the dream so they can change the ending or outcome, but there are many other ways to do this. In a journal, the dreamer can simply rewrite the ending. Instead of waking up when the monster or attacker is at your heels, consider what else you might do. You can imagine yourself successfully fighting off the attacker with a weapon or without one, if you prefer. You can tell the monster you're not afraid. These techniques work well with children who often encounter frightening figures in their dreams.

You can imagine yourself asking the attacker a question and having him answer. Knowing you're awake, you can turn to the pursuer and ask, "Who are you? What do you want?" Since all dreams come to help us and give us important information, you might be surprised at what that giant or zombie has to say. It may be a warning that something you are doing is self-destructive. One dreamer heard the monster say, "I want to help you. Learn to ask for help."

TRY THIS

Choose a dream that had an ending you didn't like. In your waking imagination, replay what led up to the last part of the dream. Then change the action to the way you'd prefer it to be. Maybe you want to chase the monster away by throwing a chair at it. Or how about waving a magic wand to turn it into a mouse? You can shout at someone who is scaring you or who is trying to intimidate you. You might yell, "GET OUT! GO AWAY!" Then ask yourself who or what this might represent in your waking life.

REQUESTS TO THE HIGHER SELF, DIALOGUING WITH HIGHER SELF

While we have talked about the Higher Self several times in this chapter, we have not yet looked at how we might address our Higher Self in a more direct way. This is the part of us where we are all more clear, wise, and aware of our complexity. The Higher Self lacks our usual hang-ups and rationalizations; it is not in denial making excuses. It sees reality as it is and knows about our potentials rather than focusing on our limiting beliefs.

For some people, the concept of having a Higher Self within them is foreign to their sense of modesty or humility. We are taught by our culture to look outside ourselves for wisdom. While we sometimes need a temporary guide or a teacher, what we often forget is that we have all the answers we need about ourselves right inside us. Overreliance on others—the clergy, experts, mentors, scientists, religious texts, parents, teachers, psychologists, counselors, doctors, psychics—for the answers to our most troubling questions is disempowering. Unlike these outsiders, we have all the facts about our experiences, talents, skills, wishes, and hopes, and we know what we need most. Learning to trust our inner knowledge is just as important as learning new skills from professionals.

TRY THIS

To access the Higher Self more directly, I suggest you imagine having a totally wise, conscious, and empathetic person available to you. You can ask this person any question at all. ABSOLUTELY ANYTHING. If it helps, imagine this person as a guru you would choose for yourself, or a wise, learned elder. Create the image in your mind in a way that has the most credibility for you. Use whatever details (male or female, human, animal, or angel, old or young, a color or light) that lead you to think of this being as having access to the ultimate Truths about you. It knows all about the universe and your place in it, your purpose here on earth. Make a list of questions you'd like to ask. There are no limitations here. Have a conversation with this guru and record this dialogue in writing. You might ask, "What is my mission?" or say, "Show me what work will most fully express what I have to offer." Or you might want to ask it to open your heart to others.

Examine what this being answers. Does it speak concretely or in metaphor? Do you receive images or words? Are there several possible interpretations to what it says? When you are done, imagine this figure moving toward you and joining with you, merging with you to the core of your being. Know that it is always available to you at any time or place.

FURTHER EXPLORATION OF SUBPERSONALITIES

When people first hear about having subpersonalities, they often think of *Sybil* or *The Three Faces of Eve*. They express concern that having subpersonalities might indicate they are suffering from Multiple Personality Disorder (MPD), now called Dissociative Identity Disorder (DID) in DSM-IV (the *Diagnostic and Statistical Manual of Mental Disorders*). I am not inclined to make psychological diagnoses based on dreams at all, and I don't recommend it for others, so that is not what I'm talking about when I speak of many personalities within the dreamer.

The primary difference between subpersonalities and the separate identities of DID is that in DID, the various personalities aren't communicating very well with one another. It is a failure of integration of the self. In fugue states, the person loses time. He is unaware of various important periods in his life. He may not remember taking a trip, painting a canvas, or he may discover he has bought a car without any memory of the event. These are not the small slips of memory we all have, like deciding to call someone and then realizing we already did. These are gaps in memory that have consequences and sometimes result in problems with the law. (See *The Minds Of Billy Milligan*, by Daniel Keyes.)

Our subpersonalities, by contrast, can talk to one another. This accounts for why we so often have arguments with ourselves. My internal financial consultant might not approve of the book lover who buys more books than I can read. It may also frown on the part of me that wants to be generous and make donations.

We are all multiple or *multifaceted*, which sounds a lot better. This aspect of being human is adaptive. To have different ways of responding and being in the world as necessary gives us an ability to act appropriately and effectively in different settings. Most of us think of these different aspects as the roles we play. The way a woman acts in front of her children will be different from her behavior as a CEO or when she is alone with her mate. The way a man acts with his buddies on the tennis court will be different from how he will be in church or when he is with a lover. Even when each of us is alone, we have various subpersonalities that may be operating at various times. Sometimes we are concentrating and serious, at other times playful and frivolous. We all talk to ourselves, no matter how embarrassed we are when others catch us doing it.

For some of us, allowing subpersonalities to show has been discouraged. If I'm an adult, when can I be silly and playful without looking foolish or risking loss of respect, or feeling like I'm wasting time? In recent years, talking about one's inner child has become part of mainstream speech, but Roberto Assagioli reminds us there are many of these subpersonalities. Subpersonalities are aspects of the Self that get little or no expression while we are playing our "proper" roles. If you become an entrepreneur and a sensible businesswoman, you may feel as if you are no longer free to take time to bake bread and make fresh vegetable soup. But many of us have a homebody personality who wants to do just that. We also have subpersonalities who need solitude, to be close to nature, to be sensual and sexual in novel ways. All these subpersonalities need to have their needs met or they will cause problems by intruding at undesirable times.

While this may seem to be off-topic in a book about dreams, being aware of the various aspects of the self is necessary for mental health and overall happiness. It is one of the ways we can find the serenity and the deep satisfaction so often missing in our lives. Since our dream actions (or the actions of other dream characters) often surprise or scare us, dreams are an excellent way to begin to be aware of and satisfy these subpersonalities.

TRY THIS

Make a list of the subpersonalities you already know about, such as the Monk, the Whore, Bratty Kid, Daredevil, Wild Man, Swinger, Hit Man, Ballerina. You might recall the Halloween costumes you've worn as expressions of some of your subpersonalities. What do you do to nurture and satisfy these parts of yourself?

TRY THIS

From one of your recent dreams, make a list of characters. See how each of these is a subpersonality of you.

THE SHADOW

The Shadow embodies those parts of ourselves we wish to deny or disown. Each of us has aspects that we find we don't like or are afraid others won't like. We don't want to see ourselves in full rage—it is too frightening. We fear the killer in us, though we all have one. We would rather say we are not like that at all. Ram Dass suggests that when we see the appalling behavior of others, we find the compassion and wisdom to say, "I am that, too."

OWNING YOUR OWN SHADOW

Instead, we are more comfortable seeing ourselves as victims of dark forces outside of us. If, in a dream, you are being chased by a big, scary person of another race or ethnic group, how is this really you? More important, how is this projection of your Shadow onto another race expressed in your waking prejudices against others? Those parts of ourselves that we can't live with, can't own, and can't be angry with, as well as those injuries and wounds inflicted by those we love, are often the very characteristics we project onto "foreigners" of all sorts. It is those bad people who do immoral things, who steal, kill, lust, and are sexually perverted. They are filthy, greedy, rude, loud, dishonest. *Certainly not us or our kind.*

Working with dreams tells us we all have these same desires and feelings. We are reminded of how we project these traits onto others. When people recognize their tendency to do this, and when they hear—in groups—the commonalties in dreams of all people, they realize how alike we all are. When we accept these parts of ourselves as part of the human condition, our tolerance and acceptance of others improve. We begin to see the folly of our racist, sexist, ageist beliefs.

This moves us beyond the personal level of dream meanings so that we can see our place in the family of humanity, in nature, and in the universe. Our dreams, especially the ones in which we see the archetypal images of Father, Mother, Wise Old Woman, and others, bring us to a place of unity that may be new for some of us. Many people feel separate, apart, and different from others. They feel out of place, unwanted, or alien. An awareness that this, too, is part of being human makes us less critical of ourselves. We understand that everyone sometimes feels as if he or she doesn't belong. For some, this sense of being alien or unwanted shows up in dreams as Shadow figures. Those parts of ourselves that we fear will be unacceptable to others are shelved and hidden away.

However, Carl Jung reminded us of the value of the Shadow. When we use so much energy to keep down parts of ourselves, we also lose a lot of our vitality and creativity that is attached to these parts. You can't shut off your awareness and feelings selectively. When you go numb to protect yourself, that numbness takes its toll on the other areas of your life. It will dull your ability to enjoy, to respond, to have enthusiasm and joy.

So what do we do with these parts of ourselves we call our Shadow? We can refuse to face them or pretend they don't exist. There are those who believe that being a spiritual person or a psychologically healthy person means that you won't ever have mean thoughts or impulses. We tell ourselves we are happy with the successes of others and don't allow ourselves our jealousies and petty envy. We think we are above such shallow and immature feelings, but they are still there. Pushed out of awareness, they may rise in a hostile comment from our lips or an unexpected small cruelty. We wonder, "Who said that?" "Who did that?" "That was *so* unlike me."

There is often a mistaken belief that we will act on feelings because we are aware of them, or that it will be too painful to feel the feelings. However, if we allow ourselves to feel these feelings, we acknowledge our humanity and can choose our behavior consciously because we are aware of these impulses before we act on them. That energy can then be rechannelled or transformed into more constructive ways of being. This is part of living a self-disciplined life and that includes not doing some things we'd like to do and doing others that are necessary and responsible. John A. Sanford (quoted in Zweig and Abrams, 1991) says "a confrontation with the Shadow is essential for self-awareness."

Jung reminds us that the Shadow is 90 percent gold. When we repress these parts of ourselves, we are using energy that could be better expended in creative living and loving. When we repress, we give up the joys as well as the pain. More dangerously, perhaps, is that we project these parts of ourselves onto others; we see the evil that exists in ourselves projected onto those we don't like and those we fear. When we stop lying to ourselves about ourselves, we are in a better position to have honest human relationships as well as being more fully who we are.

To tap into this wellspring of energy and creativity, the Shadow must be integrated—once again made part of who we truly are—and dreamwork is one way to reveal the Shadow.

WHAT IS LUCID DREAMING?

The experience of knowing you were having a dream while it was taking place is known as *lucid dreaming*. The advantage of this ability is that we are able to exercise some control over the content of our dreams. If a dreamer is being chased by a monster and he knows that he's dreaming, he can turn the monster into a mouse. Or, he can turn to the monster and ask who he is and what he wants. The answers dream figures give astonish me with their wisdom and clarity. Once again, they come to tell us what we need to hear about our mental, physical, or spiritual health. They will tell you about your addiction or your alcoholism or other self-destructive behavior. The effect on the dreamer is frequently profound.

At one workshop, a recovering addict voiced a worry that she could manipulate a lucid dream to fool herself and thereby get around the helpful and health-directing qualities of the dream. I asked her if she had ever had a dream about using drugs again, and she said yes. "How did you feel in the dreams?" I asked. She replied, "I hated myself for getting back into drugs." "And when you woke up?" I asked. "When I woke up, I was so glad it was only a dream."

So the dream reinforces her strength to stay off drugs even though she still sometimes wants to do otherwise. I don't believe a dream will ever steer us wrong, even if we are lucid and can alter the outcome of the dream. On the contrary, being lucid gives us the opportunity to overcome the monsters in our dreams and to ask them questions because we know we're really still safe asleep in our beds. Then, without fear, we can hear the messages the dreams have for us.

If you recall and record and work on your dreams on a regular basis, you will sometimes have lucid dreams. Most often, this will happen with some recurrent dream or theme that the dreamer recognizes. He thinks, "I've had this dream before!" and then— "Oh! This must be a dream, too." Or some other aspect of the dream will seem particularly strange, and the dreamer will say, "If my dead grandmother is talking to me, then I must be dreaming." But often, even knowing in the dream that someone is already dead is not enough for the dreamer to realize he's not awake.

There are several ways you can induce lucid dreaming, but you may find this difficult unless you've been working regularly with dreams for some time. This is more advanced dreamwork, and most people rarely dream lucidly.

One way to induce a lucid dream is to give yourself some task to do in the dream. This might be something simple like looking at your hands or taking off your glasses. Tell yourself that the next time you are in a nightmare, you will perform this gesture and then know you're dreaming.

LUCID DREAMING, LUCID LIVING

Some dreamworkers suggest that you ask yourself while you're *awake*, "Is this a dream? Am I dreaming now?" Asking these questions regularly while awake will increase the likelihood that you'll ask them during a dream. This also encourages a consciousness on the part of the dreamer to look for details, to notice and feel the surroundings. When they appear unreal or impossible, you will know you're dreaming. The philosopher and teacher G. I. Gurdjieff taught that most of us are dreaming most of the time, not truly awake or aware at all as we go through the motions of our days on autopilot. By asking yourself if you are dreaming, you become more conscious on a regular basis. This practice also helps us to be more mindful and lucid in our waking life.

Jeremy Taylor, in *Where People Fly and Water Runs Uphill* comments further:

> This spiritual understanding that "awakening" in the midst of dreaming is the primary means to enlightenment is shared by many Buddhist sects. In many of these traditions, this understanding leads to a belief that all living and life itself "is but a dream" and has "no true substance." This is the origin of the Buddhist theological assertion that "all is void, and without substance, like a dream." For many Buddhists, this is not simply a poetic analogy, but an absolutely accurate, technically sound, diagnostic statement of the human condition. For this reason, the ability to become more conscious and self-aware in the "dream state" (understanding that for many Buddhists, this includes all of waking life as well) is the single most important spiritual discipline that can be undertaken. (1992)

Stephen LaBerge (1990) suggests making a list of your dream signs. All of us have certain images or actions that appear regularly in our dreams. Making a list of these and being aware of them as dream signs will increase the likelihood of becoming conscious in a dream.

Some dream signs of mine and those collected from people in dream groups are listed below.

1. My car is out of control or going sideways.

2. Mom and/or Dad appears in the dream and in fact they are deceased.

3. My dogs are transformed. They look different: bigger or more muscular.

4. Dogs demonstrate some unusual behavior; e.g., My dog, Bambi, is swimming underwater; Bambi speaks and orders a daiquiri at a lunch counter.

5. I am flying like Superman or zooming along vertically with my feet not touching the ground.

6. I am in my childhood home.

7. My house is undergoing major reconstruction.

8. I am inappropriately dressed or undressed.

9. I find extra rooms, closets, or a basement in my house (no basements in Florida).

10. I am riding my bicycle cross-country.

11. Feelings of terror, panic, mortal danger.

12. Dangerous animals are threatening me.

13. Monsters are present and/or they are chasing me.

14. I am being abducted, kidnapped, or carried off.

15. Someone is breaking into my house. The alarm system doesn't work.

16. Can't find a classroom or don't know my class schedule.

17. I have to take a test I'm not prepared for, usually a final exam.

18. My movements are in slow motion.

19. I'm trying to run or scream and I can't.

20. I have goo in my mouth and around my teeth, which I extract in big globs, but there is always more and more.

21. I'm in the ocean and big waves are crashing over my head.

22. I'm using public toilets that are dirty, or people are watching or the stalls are too small for my body. Sometimes the toilets don't work or I don't have change for pay stalls.

23. I have long hair again.

24. I have a penis in my dream (from a woman).

Some of these are common dream themes, which we will discuss for their personal meanings in chapter 9. However, being able to be aware of your dream signs will help you recognize one when it appears in a dream.

Harary and Weintraub (1989) suggest choosing a lucidity symbol. This could be any item you have or something that speaks to your unconscious in a dreamlike way. You might want to choose one of your common dream signs. If you dream often about frogs, perhaps a ceramic frog will be your personal lucidity symbol. Using the symbol doesn't mean you're asking to dream about this particular symbol. Rather, it is a reminder or a cue to have a lucid dream. At bedtime, by keeping this symbol in your field of vision, you will remind yourself that you will dream lucidly.

We are most likely to become lucid during flying dreams and

recurrent dreams. We might think, "If I'm moving like this, I must be dreaming. I know I can't fly without a plane when I'm awake."

▪ STEPS FOR LUCID DREAMING ▪

1. While awake, make a habit of checking your reality by asking yourself, "Is this a dream?" "Am I dreaming now?"

2. Routinely, make a habit to look for inconsistencies or bizarre details in your surroundings. Talking animals or humans breathing underwater without scuba gear are hints that you're dreaming.

3. In a dream or a dreamlike situation, ask yourself, "Does this feel familiar?" "Have I ever dreamed this before?"

4. Ask yourself: "Could these events really happen?"

5. Tell yourself you will recognize you are dreaming in the midst of your next dream. Remind yourself of this expectation throughout the day; repeat it to yourself as you drift off to sleep.

6. Know that when you are lucid you will be able to alter the content of your dreams. Imagine yourself doing this.

7. Notice your dream signs such as: If these people are dead, then I must be dreaming!

8. Look at your transportation. If you're flying without a plane, you're dreaming!

9. Do you communicate telepathically with others, without the need to speak? This is often the method of communication in dreams.

10. Try to read something (a street sign, a movie marquis, or a book title). If the words change on a second reading, you're dreaming.

Most important:

11. Expect to be lucid the next time you are dreaming.

TRUST THE PROCESS

With any of these exercises, it is important to remember to trust the process. If you worry about the outcome, what you'll find out about yourself, or whether this or that is normal, you will miss having some of the best adventures of your lifetime. Let yourself be loose and remember that anything you write in your journal is completely private and for your eyes only. It is also only a snapshot of the moment you are writing about, not a global statement engraved in stone of who you are and the kind of person you really are. We are all many different people at different times. Doing dreamwork is one way to have access to all these strengths, talents, skills, and energies. After the first feelings of discomfort or foolishness, you will find some instructive piece of information, encouragement, or clarity.

If working with your dreams alone feels too difficult, you might try working on your dreams with the help of others.

six

Working with Dreams in Groups and with Partners

IN MY EXPERIENCE, ONE EXCELLENT WAY TO work with dreams is in a group setting. You might choose a dream partner or be part of a small group. Each has its advantages and disadvantages.

WORKING WITH DREAMS IN GROUPS

In doing dreamwork in a group, it is very important to set a tone that will facilitate the group members' telling their dreams openly and revealing their associations, fears, and concerns about the dream. The feeling of safety that comes from a group working with respect and consideration of each member takes time to establish. But the mood and tone that will allow a feeling of safety to develop must start with the first meeting. Whether you have a group leader or take turns facilitating, the norms and expectations for this particular group should be stated explicitly and restated each time a new member is added and as old ones drop out.

I will give some suggestions for these norms based on what

has worked for me, but you may want to add others as you have experience in your particular group. Bringing up discomforts and concerns is most important so that changes can be made to keep the group cohesive: that is, to maintain a feeling of comfort and safety.

I don't mean to suggest that people shouldn't ever be uncomfortable in a dream group. On the contrary, it is in the nature of dreamwork that those areas just outside our consciousness will be most likely to make us uncomfortable. It is where we are able to grow and get to know ourselves better. But the atmosphere must allow our vulnerabilities to be exposed. We should be able to talk about memories that plague us, those times when we felt ashamed or embarrassed, were dishonest and selfish. Our lust, anger, expansive generosity, greed, talents, and optimism must be allowed to show and be seen by others. This is the place for a little grandiosity—to verbalize our outrageous hopes. Working with a group, with each of us being only human, should be an occasion where our humanity can be revealed—at its best and worst.

The setting the group chooses impacts on how open the group may be. This means the group should have enough privacy that only the members are able to hear what is discussed. I believe the best dreamwork can be done when there are no restrictions placed on language or content, no taboos on subject matter. Occasionally, that will mean that people who are gay or bisexual will want and need to come out to the group so that they can properly examine the content of their dreams. Fearing the reaction of other group members, a judgment or negative reaction will inhibit effective dreamwork and undermine the stability of the group. I strongly believe gays and lesbians must be accepted into a dream group without feeling their behavior or lifestyle will be criticized. If they have the usual cautions and fears they might have in the public sector, this will create a tension that will inhibit all the group members in addition to the gay individual from getting the most from the dreams shared.

I've used the expression "to come out" as it is usually used in the gay community, but I think the term can be used with a broader scope of meaning. I think people are coming out whenever they reveal something that is a secret for them. Often, this may be some historical event such as having spent time in treatment as an in- or out-patient in a mental facility or having an illness that they are ashamed of: epilepsy, obsessive-compulsive disorder, herpes, or AIDS are a few that come to mind. A history of a clash with the justice system may be another's secret. Time spent in jail or having been accused of a crime and brought to trial are other possibilities—even if the jury found you not guilty. Other issues might be losing custody of your children, having an abortion, stealing money or information from your employer, taking medication, being the sufferer or perpetrator of abuse, taking drugs or being alcoholic in the past or present. We are not eager to tell our secrets in public. Sometimes we don't tell them to those we say we are most close to.

Additionally, people often hesitate to come out about their beliefs and how these impact on the way they run their lives. I know of one woman who strongly believes in reincarnation. She felt that many of her dreams were of unresolved issues from a previous lifetime. Realizing these issues impacted on her present life and her marriage, she wanted to discuss them. However, it took her a while to feel she could talk about this without expecting that certain members of the group would think she was crazy. My emphasis was that, whether or not we agreed with the belief in reincarnation, we could discuss these dreams with her and what they might mean in her life now.

People with unconventional beliefs and lifestyles may feel isolated and fearful about revealing themselves. How safe is it to say that you believe a monogamous relationship is impossible for you? Can you say you dislike children, hate animals, oppose abortion, prefer group sex, are a socialist, plan to accumulate wealth and have servants, or you have a gun collection? If your personal be-

liefs and life choices are out of synch with the times and culture, you may be fearful to be honest about them. A dream group should be a place where these views can be revealed without fear of attack or condemnation. That doesn't mean that you persuade one another to agree or even to see it the way you do, but rather that the dream group is a safe setting to disclose these personal views or behaviors in an open forum for expressing conflicting ideas. And for that reason, a dream group is a place to receive a most uncommon education. This is part of dreaming your real self in its most practical form. Remember, the clash of voices is the sound of freedom.

At the same time, I want to make it clear that I try not to pressure people to reveal personal material they don't want to disclose. Only the dreamer can decide if he or she feels safe enough to tell all that is relevant to a particular dream. If the dreamer makes a connection and has an *aha,* we'll see the recognition revealed in the facial expression before the dreamer reveals the content. We can know that we've hit on one meaning that resonates, but sharing that meaning and its context is up to the dreamer. I encourage such sharing, but it is not a requirement. Over time, people will naturally feel more and more comfortable about sharing their personal associations and meanings. If they do not, then the group may have grown stale with its own unspoken restrictions about what is acceptable for discussion.

When working in a group, I follow some of the suggestions for structuring a group written about by Jeremy Taylor in *Where People Fly and Water Runs Uphill* (1992). We begin the group with a touch-in, or check-in. Each person brings the group up to date on anything he or she would like to disclose and says what feelings are prominent. Since several people who come to my ongoing groups are artists or writers, I encourage them to celebrate their successes in the group, to bring their work to show and share. These have included a painting, a quilt, an embroidered blouse, a copy of an article in print. We use the group for support and en-

couragement on any projects, creative or otherwise. This is usually part of check-in. When each person has finished speaking, she turns to the next person and lets him know she's done, perhaps by saying "check," so a pause isn't misinterpreted as the end of their check-in.

After this round, we hold hands in a circle and breathe together. I sometimes use the meditation of the white light (see Appendix S) or some other visualization that helps to center the group and give us a feeling of community. This period also calms us and delineates the dream group time from our regular day. Dreamwork is a special time. A short meditation of about two to three minutes tells the participants consciously and unconsciously that this time is separate and special. Some groups prefer silent meditation so that each individual may use his or her own visualizations or prayers during that time. How you make the transition will vary based on the needs and desires of the group or the mood of that particular meeting.

The next segment is dream-sharing. The members bring a recent, recorded dream, written down right after having had the dream. Each person tells or reads a dream aloud without offering possible meanings, associations, or comments. The dream is told quickly and without elaboration and allowed to stand on its own. I ask that everyone share a dream, if possible. I usually ask for the most recent dream, but ultimately, it is up to the dreamer what dream to choose. The dreamer may want to pick an old dream that is especially haunting or a dream from a week or more ago that is particularly puzzling or upsetting.

Since we may actually explore only two or three dreams per meeting, not everyone gets to do a dream each time the group convenes. By telling our dreams, each of us is kept in contact with the unconscious of our fellow group members. If we don't get to tell a dream for several weeks, our recall will deteriorate. Telling our dreams, even without piecing together their meanings, seems to be helpful. There are moments of insight in this period, oohs and ahs and laughter around the circle.

As group leader, I share one of my recent dreams to demonstrate telling a dream without commenting on it. Because I charge fees to participate in the dream groups, we do not work with my dreams with any regularity. On rare occasions the group might want to stay late to do my dream or the group might be small enough that everyone can do a dream, including mine, during the group's time. This keeps us on more of an equal footing. Though I am the group leader and facilitator, I come to the group with my own difficulties with life, my own issues and troubles. Many times, I will have a dream and be as puzzled as anyone else as to why I would put these strange images together in such a bizarre story. Having the group see that I have blind spots, too, as they do, reduces their inclination to set me up as a guru and prevents the elitism so often present in therapy situations. In doing dreamwork, the medical model can be a hindrance. It is not that I am the professional and group members are the clients, but rather we are all in this together to figure out these marvelous puzzles, the poetry of our unconscious, and the messages the dreams offer. By working this way, my interpretations and suggestions are only one of many.

In small groups (of two or three) where everyone will surely get to do their dream in depth, this step of the quick-tell can be skipped. Otherwise, once everyone has told a dream briefly, we focus on individual dreams. Generally, I will suggest we do the most pressing dream first. Nightmares or other dreams that left the dreamer disquieted and uneasy take precedence. A dream group that has been together for a while will often choose which dreams to do, being careful that no dreamer is neglected for too long.

We work on each dream in detail, doing as many as time allows. My groups are usually two or two and a half hours. At least two dreams can be done in depth during that time, sometimes three. When the group is really cohesive and moves along with little resistance, we might get to do a fourth dream in a two-and-a-half-hour session. Then we close with a meditation, holding hands, and breathing together.

Sharing food and any social discussion not directly related to the dreamwork takes place after the closing breathing/meditation. We do not eat or have drinks during the dream group, with the exception of water. I believe that snacks and food distract us from the inner, psychological exploration that dreamwork makes possible.

FREQUENCY OF MEETINGS

My preference is for a once-weekly group, meeting in the same place and at the same time. Meeting less often makes it harder for the group to have a sense of unity and commitment. Unfortunately, my groups generally meet only twice-monthly and I see this as a deficit. A break of two weeks or more often means that we have a lot of catching up to do on the current events in our lives. Touch-in may take up more time than we'd like. Members sometimes feel uneasy about revealing secrets to people they see only twice a month; they can't feel close and intimate without more regular contact.

Irvin Yalom, writing about group psychotherapy (1975) states that investigating dreams in group work "would demand that a disproportionate amount of time be spent on one patient; the process would, furthermore, be minimally useful to the remaining members who would become mere bystanders."

Techniques for avoiding these pitfalls while keeping everyone involved are discussed below. However, Yalom balances this comment later in his book when he refers to ". . . observing members do some significant, silent, internal work which is instigated by some aspect of the work of another." This is especially true, I believe, when working with dreams since they speak a universal (as well as personal) language of symbol and metaphor. All of us are faced with similar life issues and can experience a moment of personal revelation or an *aha* from someone else's dream. On occasion, it is easier to have insights with someone else's dream because we seem to have fewer blind spots to someone else's dream story.

INHIBITIONS DUE TO PRESENCE OF PARTICULAR DREAM MEMBERS

In dream groups, friction among members will invariably arise. Conflict is part of life and a dream group can be an excellent place to practice resolving differences, master respecting other points of view, and learn to agree to disagree. Occasionally, one group member may inhibit another from telling a dream or explaining its possible meanings. This needs to be addressed quickly, before the dream group goes stale or deteriorates into "polite" conversation. The person facilitating the dream group can address these issues as part of setting norms for the group. A private discussion with the inhibited person might reveal what is holding him back, and this issue can be addressed more directly in the group. If one person is feeling inhibited and then holds back because of these feelings, other members of the group are also likely to be aware of this tension. The group is then at risk of a downward spiral unless the members and leader are willing to say whatever needs to be said.

MINIMUM NUMBER OF SESSIONS

I ask that anyone joining a dream group commit to a minimum number of sessions in advance. At the time of this writing, I ask for prepayment of six consecutive sessions in advance. (At twice monthly, that's three months.) There is no credit given for missed sessions (except in rare circumstances) and no refunds for dropouts. I generally ask that people let me or another group member know if someone has to miss a session.

The intent is to have a cohesive group that meets regularly and where the participants have made a serious commitment to working together as a group. People occasionally want to come to one session "to try it out" or come only when they have a dream to tell. I do not agree to such arrangements since it disrupts the equilibrium of the group to have people coming and going according to whim. Such behavior also inhibits the group from becoming cohesive and trusting. Interested individuals who do not want to do group work or hear the dreams of others are recommended to do dreamwork individually instead. I do tell them, however, that they will get much more benefit from working with the group and that it will be much less costly as well.

COMPOSITION OF THE GROUP

The decision of who is eligible to be part of a dream group is usually made by a group leader. As a therapist, I am conscious of a range of emotional and mental difficulties that might make someone less than desirable for a dream group. Narcissistic and hysterical types who have a crisis for every meeting and need to keep the group's focus on them are more suitable for a therapy group where these personality traits can be better addressed than in a dream group where people are prepared to take turns with their own dreams and be helpful to one another. Individuals who have difficulty with putting themselves aside and being empathic and interested in others are generally disruptive to a dream group. On the other hand, this could be an opportunity for them to begin to feel welcome and have a sense of community for the first time, thereby paving the way to health. A forgiving group with competent leadership can be helpful to such people, especially if the members are committed to weathering storms and the group is already cohesive. The group can gently let someone know if he or she is being disruptive, derailing the group from dreamwork into other subjects or idle chitchat, or behaving in a way that is perceived as disrespectful of specific members.

Generally speaking, people who are able to be introspective and nondefensive in their interactions are the best candidates for being part of a dream group. Having had some experience in therapy is usually an asset, but not a requirement. Because these people have already experienced examining their behavior, feelings, and taking responsibility for their lives, doing dreamwork is a natural extension of the therapy process. The exception would be those who come from a dogmatic position of what dream symbols must mean. People who have done inner work through other means including journals, self-help, support, and recovery groups are also excellent prospects for continuing their self-improvement through working with dreams.

FAMILY MEMBERS IN THE SAME GROUP

The question of whether to have family members and mates as members of the same dream group comes up frequently. Since I have several different groups in progress, I usually recommend that family members join different groups so that they can feel as uninhibited as possible about bringing up the issues in these intimate relationships. Of course, some relationships will thrive in a dream group if they are already strong and can handle the confrontations that are a natural by-product of dreamwork. This is also true if the members are not averse to "airing their dirty linen in public." If the prospect of a discussion of family secrets might be problematic for one or another of the parties, then they would do better by each being among strangers in separate groups. I feel this is more true across generations (parents and adult children in the same group) than with lovers or mates. In fact, I recommend that people tell their spouses their dreams because it is an excellent way to build intimacy. But telling someone a dream after you've spent some time working on it is different from telling it the first time (as in a dream group) while you are still uncertain of what you will reveal and how insensitively you might reveal it. This may be a consideration when close friends want to be in the same dream group, also. Those rough areas in their friendships are likely to come out in their dreams.

When asked what I suggest in this case, I'll let the person know the possible risks and benefits and let her decide whether she is as open in her marriage or friendship as she'd like to be in the dream group. If the relationship is already committed to honesty and integrity, then dreamwork will facilitate those qualities.

ASSEMBLING YOUR OWN DREAM GROUP

If, after reading this book and the others recommended in the bibliography, you'd like to start a dream group on your own, you could ask people who you feel might be interested in joining you. It is not necessary to have a psychologist or therapist present if working with dreams is entered into in a spirit of support and cooperation. Jeremy Taylor (1992) says it well: "The cleverest and most perceptive dream work undertaken with secret internal cynicism and disrespect for others will be counterproductive, while the most naive and blundering work with dreams, undertaken with wholeheartedness and openness, will be profoundly useful."

When choosing members of your group, keep in mind those traits listed below for choosing a dream partner.

CONFIDENTIALITY

Members in dream groups must be cautioned that the content of all the dream groups and what comes out of dreamwork is always confidential. (See Norms for Dream Groups in Appendix N) Members are asked not to reveal to their mates or friends the outcome of dreamwork or the secrets revealed to anyone outside the group. I read the norms aloud when new members join the group.

GROUP TECHNIQUES

In addition to all the techniques discussed in this book, working in a group affords the dreamer the opportunity of hearing other people's thoughts on and reactions to the dream. Rather than waiting for a turn to tell a dream, I suggest that group members listen to each dream as if it were their own. I give this instruction at the beginning of a group and each time a new person is added. I suggest, "Listen to this dream as if it were yours. Instead of just listening with your intellectual minds and applying what you've read about dream symbols in books, I want you to listen with your hearts and your feelings. What would this dream be about if it were your dream and how would you feel about it? Would you feel the same way as the dreamer? What does this dream call up for you? What emotions and what memories? What does the dream ending say about you?"

This encourages the other group members to be fully engaged with the dreamer. We enter into the person's dream and try to experience it personally and emotionally instead of abstractly or intellectually. This not only fosters empathy and camaraderie within the group but also makes each dream personally meaningful to all the group members. We may each have an *aha* for every dream told. One woman said that each dream group is very meaningful to her, whether or not she tells a dream. Each time, she said she comes away with the same feeling she had experienced after her most important individual therapy sessions. At home, there was much to mull over and digest and many feelings brought to the surface. We all face many of the same issues in our lives, and dreamwork is a constant reminder of our similarities.

Remembering that anything anyone other than the dreamer says about a dream can only be a projection of the speaker's issues, group members are asked to respond to the dream as if it were their dream. I am fairly insistent that each person begin the sentence with, "If it were my dream . . ." I say, explicitly, that they are not to begin a sentence with "You . . ." This prevents group members from telling the dreamer what his or her dream means in a dogmatic and authoritarian style and helps maintain the supportive and nonjudgmental tone of the group. A group that has been in progress for a while might begin to say things like "Maybe this is a dream about your wanting your child to be more like other children." Such tentative and respectful interpretations are appropriate once the group has been through a period of work together that has eliminated the problems of members trying to tell one another what or how to be. Still, the best safeguard against this deterioration is to maintain the rule that each sentence begin with "If it were my dream . . ." (Taylor, 1992; Ullman, Montague, and Zimmerman, 1979). Another advantage of using this construction is that each time someone truly explores a dream from this perspective, there is the opportunity for the speaker to discover something about him- or herself. Frequently, I and other members of a group will have deep and important insights when doing this.

In one dream group, a man told of watching a jumbo jet, a 747, coming in for a landing right over his car. As he watched, he saw that a royal palm tree was hanging off the tail of the plane and he was certain that this was going to cause the plane to crash. For him, a royal palm tree was a symbol of wealth, success, status. He said, royal palms are expensive additions to landscaping, they are the tallest and heaviest of palm trees, and they are seen on the estates of wealthy people. The plane was weighted down by the tree, however, which was the cause of the crash. He felt that this was telling him that his devotion to money was the cause of his previous crash (bankruptcy) and could be a warning about a future crash if he took another job with the hope of getting rich quickly. The dream ended with his telling a young woman how blessed she was to have survived the crash and that she must have important work to do.

For the dreamer, this was about clarifying his values of looking for quick wealth versus making a slow and steady pace in a more stable field of work. It was about not letting his greed interfere with his spiritual growth. On another level, it was about his struggle with alcohol and how that might hold him back from future success or result in another crash.

The other group members responded wholeheartedly to this image. I, too, felt this was an image that resonated with my own life. What was I hanging on to that was holding me down or holding me back in my life? What was keeping me from flying/soaring? What might cause a crash if I didn't let go of it? Using this man's dream, each of the participants in this group was able to explore what might be weighing us down. As a metaphor, it leaves a lot of room for each of us to put our own personal slant on it. Even the "weighted down" phrase made some think of how actual physical weight might have become a barrier to good health or social opportunities.

As a group leader, in addition to setting the tone and teaching techniques by example, I want to be sure each member is involved. By watching each person, I can see when someone has had an *aha*. I encourage sharing these thoughts and insights. I ask the more introverted members if they want to add something or make a comment. A synergy is created: the combined energies, thoughts, and insights of the group are much greater than what any one dreamer might have accomplished when working alone. One thought leads to others. One person's insight, especially if it comes with a difficult admission or recognition, will lead others to a similar experience. At times, everyone seems to make a connection with the dream's meaning at once and the group gasps in unison. "WOW!" we all say together. At other times, we have simultaneous laughter or tears.

One of the significant advantages of doing dreamwork in a

group is that it dilutes the power of the therapist/facilitator. As a group leader, I come to my understanding of a dream through my own education, experience, culture, expectations, just as every other person does. No matter how well informed and experienced I may be, I am still a limited individual with a narrow focus. No matter how much I try to overcome my limitations, I am limited. If I were the only person to ask questions of the dreamer, to suggest possible interpretations and ways of looking at the dream as metaphor, those would be the only ones the dreamer would hear.

DREAM PARTNERS

Earlier, I made reference to my having a dream partner. This is a good friend whom I talk to frequently. We share dreams with each other and because we know each other's issues, we can quickly hear the metaphors in each other's dreams. I have worked with my dreams a long time; but, like everyone else, I have my blind spots. Just as you do, I sometimes kid myself or make excuses. My dream partner knows not only what is going on in my life at present but also my history, in excruciating detail, as I know hers. My dreams will frequently have references to childhood events, traumas, secrets I share with few people, but because I have either already shared these with her or am willing to, we can get to the meanings of the dreams without my worrying about what subjects might be taboo in this relationship.

The information in my dreams can set me straight. Still, I might not understand what they mean without someone asking me for the descriptions of details and the feelings. I, too, need to be prompted to make the bridges because of the temptation to see only the quick and simple interpretation. Working together with a dream partner over a long period of time, we are likely to hear patterns and recurrent themes in each other's dreams more than in our own.

When you pick a dream partner, choose someone who will respect your process and your privacy. You'll want a partner who can respect your view of the world and your life choices—especially when they differ from your partner's view.

Your dream partner should be a good listener and ask questions more than trying to provide answers for you. Only the dreamer is the real authority on the dream's meaning. As I said, anything anyone else says about your dream can only be a projection of that person's issues onto your dream—no different from reading inkblots. Listen to your inner voice and ask yourself if this person's comment feels right *for you.*

Regularly working with others on dreams—theirs and ours—brings greater intimacy and understanding among people. Sometimes, we can best say what troubles us to another person by telling a dream. The person hears the metaphor and often will see himself as the monster or the attacker without having to be told. This opens up a communication that might have been difficult if approached more directly. By sharing dreams, we expose our innermost thoughts and feelings to one another, bringing each of us closer to wholeness and acceptance. By hearing another's dream, we come to know the dreamer more deeply. Dream sharing is one unconscious speaking to another.

Even if we don't understand a dream, the simple act of listening with attention and respect is helpful. Just as unremembered dreams do their work for us, dreams told but not analyzed can be therapeutic or comforting. Having someone listen attentively to anything we say feels good. It validates our existence and our sense of personal value. This is true of children's dreams, too. Paying attention to another without judgment is an excellent gift whether it is to a child or an adult.

·*seven*·

Recurrent Dreams, Recurrent Themes, and Nightmares

WHY WE HAVE RECURRENT DREAMS

People who come to me with an interest in their dreams often do so because they have had a recurrent dream or recurrent nightmare for years or decades. They want the dream to stop. They think by telling me the dream I will be able to make it stop. Just like that. They don't want to know what it means; they just want to be free of this continuous loop of dreaming each night. First I have to tell them that their dream is a message they haven't been heeding and they need to find out what the message is. Some people would prefer to take a pill to stop the dreams, but this doesn't make the issue go away. It only buries it deeper and then each time it surfaces, it is more powerful. Though time is a great healer, the best way to deal with a problem is to face it with courage and confidence.

A CALL TO ACTION

When a dreamer has a dream in the same form over and over, the unconscious is saying, "This is the best way I know how to tell you this. These are the most perfect symbols for what you need to know now. I'm going to tell you this over and over until you get it!" The dream will continue to repeat until you do whatever needs to be done, until you take action. This is probably true for most dreams, but a recurrent dream is more insistent. It is a call to arms. It's time to change what the dream is telling you to change. Side-stepping the issue includes the risk of holding on to some unresolved issues that may be diminishing our effectiveness in living.

This doesn't necessarily mean a dramatic change, but it sometimes does. Perhaps you have been trying to fix something that can't be fixed: a job or a relationship or a health problem you have to live with and accept. Perhaps you have been unwilling to take a hard look at your own behavior or you're neglecting your deteriorating health and it's time to do something different. Just as often, the action may only be a change in perspective or the way you've been handling a current problem. Many things can't be changed. Maturity sometimes means the ability to accept what cannot be changed with equanimity.

If the dreamer has difficulty understanding the dream's message, he can always ask for another dream for clarification or elaboration. You might incubate a new dream by writing in your journal something like "Okay. I know this is important information, but I'm not getting it. Can you tell me this in another way? May I have a dream that will be clear to me?" And see what you receive.

When you do dreamwork regularly through dream diaries or in a dream group, you will be able to see your dreams as a series that has a natural progression. In the big picture, your dreams will reflect your growth and improved understanding along your life path. You will also see that certain dreams reappear at certain times in your life, often during stress or times of significant change.

STEPS FOR WORKING WITH RECURRENT DREAMS

If you have a recurrent dream, the first thing you want to pay attention to is when the dream comes. I will always ask dreamers, "When did you first have this dream?" Much to my surprise, they can usually pinpoint the first time the dream appeared. If they cannot pinpoint a specific time such as a date or a school grade, they can often place it in time with another important life event. The dreamer might say, "It started about the time I got married." Or, "I had the dream for the first time just before I graduated from high school." *This is important information.* When the dream started is an indication of a change in the person's life (or perspective on life) that is reflected in the dream's symbols.

Then I ask, "When was the last time you had the dream?"

This might be harder to pinpoint, unless this is a dream the person has very frequently. More often, a recurrent dream comes once a month or less, but of course, this is highly variable, depending on what the dream means and its emotional impact on the dreamer.

Placing the first occurrence of the dream alongside the last occurrence of the dream is the beginning of seeing the pattern of when the dream comes. The dream might be a way of telling you when you are feeling stressed or overworked or need to change something in the way you're conducting your life. Since we are all guilty of making many of the same mistakes several times in our lives, often the dream comes as a reminder that we're doing that same old thing over again. It may only be that we're making the same cognitive mistake, but certainly, what is happening in our life is a repeat in some way and so the dream comes in its old form to tell us that. Try to find the pattern in the occurrence of your dream.

One woman in a dream group told of a recurrent nightmare she'd had for many, many years. The image was of an old, sick man in a hospital bed. He had a cane or an umbrella and was trying to catch her with the hook at the end of it. This was a terrifying dream for this grown woman in her fifties.

In answer to the question of when the dream started, this woman said, without any hesitation, "In the second grade." I asked, "What happened in the second grade of special significance to you?" Again, she answered quickly. "My grandfather died." Without knowing any more, I wondered silently whether this dream had to do with death in some way even though she didn't say she feared death when the dream came to her. Of course, I might be wrong and only the dreamer can confirm or refute a suggested interpretation.

When I asked her when she last had the dream, she was more vague. "I haven't had it for a while. I guess I had it about nine months ago." I waited for her to make her own connection, but I didn't see the visible facial reaction I was waiting for. I asked, "What was happening in your life nine months ago?" "Nothing." Her face showed no recognition.

This was a private dream group of twelve women, most of whom knew one another, all friends of the hostess who had hired me for the group. A second woman sitting next to the dreamer reacted strongly by staring at the dreamer. "Do you want to say something?" The second woman responded without taking her eyes off the dreamer. "Nine months ago, you had a lump on your breast!"

"Oh!"

There was the reaction I had expected. Sometimes I don't see the dreamer make this connection because it happens later or the next day outside of my presence.

"Yes!" She turned to me. "The lump was benign, but I was scared."

The entire group had an *aha* at that point. This dream was recurrent and most likely came to the dreamer when she was faced with issues of mortality. The first time was when she had to deal with her grandfather's death and the last time with the imminent possibility of her own death. Knowing this was a possible pattern, I suggested that the dreamer pay attention when the dream comes again and see what is happening in her life that might point to an issue of mortality—literal or metaphorical. (We say people are killing us, but we don't usually mean physical death.) This dream-work greatly reassured the dreamer and took away the terror this dream brought with it.

If the dreamer can't recall any specific event at the time of the dream, but can place it in time, I ask what her life was like at that time. Often a detail in the dream will bring up associations with a particular time and I will ask what life was like at that time. What were the predominant feelings in that era? Was she happy? Unhappy? Exciting? Optimistic? In love? At the end of a relationship? If yes, by whose decision?

Perhaps the dream recurs when present life circumstances create feelings similar to that earlier time. If the dreamer is driving a car he hasn't had in many years, I ask him what his life was like at the time when he owned that particular car. Perhaps it was before he was married and had the responsibilities of a family, which he sometimes feels is a burden. Or perhaps he had the car before his divorce and he misses the family life he had that the car has come to represent in his dreams.

RECURRENT THEMES

Another reason we have recurrent dreams is that the unconscious seems to like the same symbols and themes. Because they capture a feeling, an idea, or a person so well, we use them over and over again. Some of these recurrent dreams and themes will show up in many people's dreams because they represent common figures of speech or common symbols in the culture. This recurrent "killing me" dream pattern has become a favorite metaphor in dreams, and one of several favorites. I've already mentioned how my dream of being back working in a hospital laboratory comes when I am feeling stressed out and unappreciated. More often than not, I am creating the situation and I know I can change it.

In this case, the dream itself is not to be seen as a problem, but rather as a sort of barometer for a life pattern. In my case, the dream warns me to get some rest, to not take myself so seriously. Perhaps your recurrent dream or theme does something similar for you.

Once you've established when the dream appears, then you are well on the way to understanding the message. Ask yourself the usual dream questions we touch on throughout this book: What are the feelings? How are the feelings in my life similar to the ones in the dream? Examine your associations to each of the dream elements.

Once again, remember that a recurrent dream, like any dream, is about what is happening to you now. If you've used the metaphor of driving a car to represent how you are running your life, this dream theme may continue even though you may no longer drive. If, at the time you were building a home, you began to use the metaphor of fixing up a house to represent your concerns about the physical health of your body, you might continue to use this metaphor long after you moved to an apartment or onto a houseboat. The metaphor works for our unconscious and we continue to use it even though we recognize it as a symbol.

SPECIAL MEANINGS

Though a recurrent dream may appear nearly the same each time, there are usually subtle differences in the plot or actions of the dream. These will be the clues to arrive at the current meaning of the dream—what you need to know *now*, which might be different from what the dream meant when you had it a few months ago.

As an example, the metaphor of being in over your head, a common figure of speech and a common feeling, might be symbolized as drowning or being unable to touch bottom in a pool. At one time, this might represent feeling overwhelmed with work responsibilities. At another time, the dreamer might feel this is more related to a problem in a personal relationship. Perhaps the person has the feeling of not being up to the demands or expectations of the other person.

In chapter 9, we'll look at common dream themes. Any one or several of these might show up repeatedly as a recurrent dream for a particular dreamer. Unless the dream is disturbing and you want relief from the dream feelings and their aftermath, consider your recurrent dream your own personal shorthand for a particular statement about your life.

NIGHTMARES
WHAT ARE NIGHTMARES?

For most people a dream is called a nightmare when they wake up frightened by its content. Nightmares seem particularly vivid and lifelike. The circumstances are frequently life threatening, such as a monster or person chasing them with the intent to kill. Or the threat is extremely upsetting because it is the loss of a loved one, a humiliating experience, or the perceived threat to something they value. The dreamer is likely to call a dream a nightmare if he wakes up sweating, with a pounding heart, or wakes himself as he tried to scream. If the dreamer is crying in the dream and wakes up and continues to cry or has other unpleasant feelings linger for some time after the dream, she is likely to refer to the experience as a nightmare.

WHO HAS NIGHTMARES?

Anyone can have nightmares. They are not reserved for any particular group and they do not mean you have a mental illness or emotional instability. The nightmare is the dream you need at this time you have it to tell you what you need to know. That it comes in neon lights with Stephen Spielberg special effects is only a message more insistently delivered. Sometimes, a recurrent dream whose message is not addressed will escalate into a nightmare if the dreamer doesn't take the action indicated by the message of the dream.

The frequency and duration of nightmares varies widely from person to person. Some people have nightmares several times a week and some report having them only rarely, or never having had one since childhood or adolescence. Since what people describe as a nightmare will also determine whether they say they have one, it becomes hard to get data on who has nightmares and who doesn't. I have heard people tell dreams that I would have called nightmares if I had had them, but the dreamers maintained these weren't nightmares for them. Though the content sounded creepy and terrifying to me and other group members, the dreamer approached the experience as an adventure or with curiosity. Perhaps some dreamers are reluctant to label their dreams as nightmares because this imparts a pathological state to them, and they avoid the word. Others will quickly refer to any unpleasant dream that disgusts them or brings up feelings of guilt, embarrassment, or frustration, like a nightmare.

Certainly, people who lead normal and productive lives are among those who have had nightmares frequently for decades (Krakow and Neidhardt, 1992). The experience of having nightmares, by itself, is no way to measure mental health or the lack of it. A single dream of a psychotic is indistinguishable from the dreams of so-called normal persons. Perhaps the difficulty here is mainly with language and common distinctions. Bill Borcherdt, author and psychotherapist, says, "I don't want to be normal; I want to be healthy."

POSSIBLE CAUSES: INSIDE OR OUT

Nightmares may be the result of a variety of causes coming from within the dreamer in addition to those outside. Most of dreamwork focuses on inner conflicts, fears, and worries, repressed emotions, and ambivalence in our relationships and choices. If these opposing inner forces create enough stress for the dreamer, they are likely to precipitate nightmares.

A traumatic event or the fear of its recurrence often causes nightmares. If you've had a car accident or your house has been burglarized, you are likely to have nightmares for a while after the event. Witnessing a violent crime or accident can be traumatic even if you suffer no physical harm yourself. Even a close call with a bad accident can start a round of anxiety or panic attacks that are repeated in dreams. If the event was very upsetting, the nightmares of the images of the calamity might continue for years, with the nightmares being one of several symptoms of posttraumatic stress disorder (PTSD). The nightmares may become a personal metaphor for stress, terror, or threats of all kinds, just as any recurring dream can act as a repeating metaphor. Through dreaming, the unconscious is trying to come to terms with the event, to finish what was unfinished, perhaps to undo the tragedy or prevent it from ever happening again. As we go over and over something in our waking minds, so do we in our sleep. Over time, the nightmare may disappear. If not, taking some new action as we discussed earlier will change or stop the nightmare. If you are indulging in some ongoing self-destructive behavior such as smoking, drinking excessively, or using drugs, the nightmare will probably continue until you make a change toward health.

SUDDEN ONSET OF NIGHTMARES

At other times, nightmares can be caused by the chemicals we take into our bodies. These can be allergic reactions to certain foods, using prescription or addictive drugs, or chemicals in our foods and our environment.

If you suddenly start having nightmares and haven't had them very often before, ask yourself what has changed in your life. If you've just begun to take a new medication, check with your doctor to see if that might be the cause. *Never change your prescription medication without consulting your physician since a sudden change in dosage could be life threatening.*

Check to see if you've changed your eating habits. If you are eating more in restaurants or more prepared foods, you might be consuming more chemical additives. Be aware of how much caffeine, sugar, or sugar substitutes you ingest and examine whether you've changed your consumption of these substances. Consider eliminating them from your diet. Also examine if there has been a change in your life in some other way. Alterations in your fluid intake, sleep pattern, sleep partner, habits, stress levels, relationships, or financial security can all lead to the onset of nightmares.

At an interpersonal level, you might want to consider any recent change in your relationships that might be reflected in the content of your nightmares. An increase in responsibilities, stress at work, even positive changes in your life can bring on nightmares as you are adapting to the changes.

SPECIAL MEANINGS

As with all dreams, you will have to look at what the nightmare is saying about your life and how the dream images and feelings correlate with your waking experiences just before the dream. Don't expect the dream to stop just because you know what it's about. You will probably have to take some action.

Just as recurrent dreams are a call to arms, so too are nightmares. A nightmare whose problem is not addressed can turn into a recurrent nightmare. Or a recurrent dream may escalate to become more and more nightmarish in the unfolding of the dream images and outcome. These dreams that leave the dreamer uncomfortable, fearful, concerned, or anxious, require action. They have a special and unique meaning for the dreamer that, when made conscious, requires action.

NIGHTMARES IN CHILDREN

Nightmares are part of the normal pattern of childhood development. We know that most children have "bad dreams" and will begin to report them as soon as they are able to express their feelings and experiences. Like adults, children dream about what is on their minds and about what troubles them. A boy who was just beginning to speak woke up crying and pointed to the mural of fish and bubbles on his bedroom wall. "Fish go boom," he said, trying to tell his mother he'd dreamed the fish fell off the wall (and onto him, presumably). Small children need to be comforted and reassured after waking from bad dreams. Let them express whatever they are able to, giving them an opportunity to get complete with these feelings. It can be helpful to demonstrate the difference between reality and the dream, perhaps by showing them something couldn't happen. For example, by letting him see that when you touch the painted fish on the wall, it doesn't come off and can't fall on him.

With older children whose dreams take on more and more symbolic imagery, you can begin doing dreamwork with any of the techniques in this book, exploring the feelings and associations to the dream images, asking them for connections with waking concerns and experiences. These questions must be appropriate to the child's age and cognitive abilities. Sometimes a child is troubled by events and hesitates to talk about them. By telling a dream, the child can open the subject more delicately or perhaps not even be consciously aware of where the dream might lead. This is an excellent opportunity for parents to begin a trusting, respectful, and open communication with children who might be more quiet otherwise. The safe space surrounding respectful dreamwork creates bonds and trust regardless of the age of the participants. A parent talking about his own dreams models the behavior that talking about dreams is a valid topic for discussion, worthy of serious scrutiny. Do not shame the child or castigate yourself for the content of dreams. This is an outlet for feelings that might not be appropriate in waking life or in certain circumstances. Teaching your child appropriate outlets for these feelings (in addition to learning them yourself) is one of the benefits of doing dreamwork as a family.

NIGHTMARES VERSUS NIGHT TERRORS

Whether adult or child, it is important to distinguish between a nightmare and a night terror, since the way one approaches the child is different for each problem. A nightmare will usually produce a spontaneous report of fearful dream images or a dream story. The child might wake up and tell the dreams while crying and distressed over the events of the dream. On the other hand, night terrors (or sleep terrors, also called *pavor nocturnus*) usually occur with little or no dream imagery. The child doesn't fully wake up and if awakened is unable to describe the experience beyond expressing fear. Waking the child and insisting on hearing about a dream he didn't have can cause more problems than exist already. The child might feel pressured to make something up or feel that something is terribly wrong with him because he can't remember what happened. In night terrors, the child may not allow you to comfort or hold him and might even push you away. If not awakened, he will also have no memory of the event in the morning. Your questioning and anxiety can add to the child's fears. It is better to remain calm in your child's presence and he will usually return to deep sleep after a few minutes. If it is a nightmare, the child will remain frightened but will usually be able to relate a dream without much prompting (see Ferber, *Solve Your Child's Sleep Problems*).

DSM-IV (*Diagnostic and Statistical Manual of Mental Disorders*, 1994) states that in children, sleep terrors are more common in males than in females. In adults, the sex ratio is even.

PREVENTION

The best way to prevent nightmares is to stay in as close contact as possible with your unconscious. This means doing inner work on a regular basis, preferably daily, through dreamwork, journal writing, creative projects, meditation, and sharing yourself with others honestly and fully as much as possible. Each time we push away an uncomfortable feeling or hold in the words we need to say, we risk having these issues bubble up in the night in horrific dream images. If we face our fears and anxieties regularly and move toward conquering them, we will be less likely to experience nightmares.

But when you have a nightmare, remember to think of it as a gift, just as all dreams are gifts. There is important information in it that you can use immediately.

SLEEPWALKING (SOMNAMBULISM)

Many children have isolated or infrequent episodes of sleepwalking, which they outgrow later in life. Both sleepwalking and sleep terrors seem to run in families, with the likelihood increasing with the incidence of other family members having these inclinations. Identical twins (from one fertilized egg) are six times more likely to both be sleepwalkers than fraternal twins (from two separately fertilized eggs). Both sleep terrors and enuresis (bedwetting) are more frequent in families with a history of sleepwalking.

Sleepwalking is potentially dangerous because of the individual's lack of waking judgment. Sleepwalkers have been known to walk off balconies, climb out of windows, leave the house and venture into traffic, step out of a moving camper vehicle on a freeway. Because of these dangers, these individuals are frequently treated with medication. In adults, sleepwalking is considered a disorder and medical intervention may be necessary to protect the sleepwalker and those whom he might assault while in this state.

Sleepwalking is also a feature of posttraumatic stress disorder

(PTSD), especially as seen in Vietnam veterans. Many persons who have been exposed to early childhood violence will experience sleep terrors and sleepwalking in their prepubertal years.

In the elderly, especially those in nursing homes, nocturnal wandering is more frequently due to disorientation as a result of diminished mental capacities than to sleepwalking.

DSM-IV (*Diagnostic and Statistical Manual of Mental Disorders,* 1994) states that violent behaviors during sleepwalking episodes are more likely in adults than in children. Sleepwalking occurs with equal frequency in both sexes.

▪ SUGGESTED PRECAUTIONS FOR SLEEPWALKERS ▪

1. Keep doors and windows locked.

2. If necessary, install a second, out-of-reach lock for children.

3. Use an alarm or bell on the bedroom door of the sleepwalker.

4. Have the sleepwalker sleep on the first floor of the home or in hotels when traveling.

5. Use protective films or heavy drapes on windows.

6. Install a home alarm system and engage the system during sleeping hours.

7. Remove dangerous items from the bedroom and home, if necessary, especially guns and knives.

8. Pair the sleepwalker with a light-sleeping roommate, if possible.

9. When dangerous behavior is associated with sleepwalking, *consult a physician* specializing in sleep disorders.

SLEEP TALKING

Sleep talking occurs at all ages, but more often in females than males. These individuals may be coherent or not, speak in fragments or full sentences. They will sometimes answer questions, though rarely. Absent other sleep disorders or disturbances, sleep talking is no cause for concern and may or may not be associated with dream content.

For more information and research on sleep problems, sleep disorders, and treatment, see *Principles and Practices of Sleep Medicine* (Kryger, Roth, and Dement, 1994).

· eight ·

Sexual and Erotic Dreams

WE ALL HAVE SEXUAL DREAMS AT MANY TIMES in our lives. These are the dreams that people are frequently reluctant to share at a workshop with strangers. Afraid of what the dream might reveal about their sexual preferences, their secret desires, or their hang-ups about sex, they wait until someone else shares a dream with sexual content. After one dream with sexual imagery has been shared, the other members are more likely to tell theirs. When we have disturbing sexual dreams that offend our waking sensibilities, we must remind ourselves the dream is a gift—if only we can take the time to get past the literalism of this graphic metaphor and see how useful the information is.

To begin our exploration of sexual dreams, I would like to note that I've observed that dreams with explicitly sexual detail are not always just about a sexual issue and those dreams that appear to be nonsexual—such as purchasing bananas at a fruit stand (see chapter 3)—can have sexual meanings. When trying to reveal the metaphors of a sexual dream, as with any dream, we look at the details and feelings. We then ask the dreamer to see how this is a metaphor for what is happening in his daily life. Sometimes dreams are a way of discharging sexual frustration and desire.

One man told a dream of having a strong sexual desire for a woman. Each time they were about to begin lovemaking, he was interrupted—first by his young son, then by his wife, then his father, and then a telephone call from work. Beyond the expression of simple sexual desire, I asked the dreamer how all these elements—wife, son, father, work—were keeping him from doing things he wanted to do. This idea resonated with the man. There were many things he couldn't do because of his obligations and commitments to others, and it sometimes troubled him. He was a responsible person who had a subpersonality who wanted to be wild and irresponsible—especially in a sexual way—but he didn't allow himself infidelity or any shirking of his duties. The desires and the obstacles to expressing this side of himself came out in his dream.

This is an example of peeling back the layers of a dream. At the surface level, this is about sexual desire for variety and satisfaction. At another level, we can see how the dream might be telling him how much he feels his life circumstances are obstacles to personal satisfaction. All choices are a trade-off. The dream reminds us that even when we put aside feelings for a greater good, they aren't gone. We must still recognize them. Sometimes, talking them out in fantasy or writing them out in storytelling is a way to give voice to those suppressed parts of ourselves. When we accept them as part of us, we don't have to use energy to keep them stuffed down.

DESIRES AND WISHES

Most people working on their dreams alone would see only the first layer of a sexual dream: I need/want sex, so I have it in my dream. They stop there and miss seeing the larger view the dream provides through using sex as a metaphor.

In working with the first and literal layer of a sexual dream, we begin with seeing the imagery as it is. If you're dreaming about sex, the meaning has value in terms of your sexual experiences or desires. I suggest looking at the literal layer first. If you've had a dream in which you have a particular sex partner, I ask, *Do you think some part of you would like to be sexual with this person?* Note that I use the phrase *some part of you.* Or I might say "on some level." Because we are all composed of several subpersonalities, one of these may be expressing a desire that the rest of you rejects. Perhaps you find someone appealing on a purely physical level, but you don't like or respect her. You know she's a nasty person, and you don't want to be around her. You feel unsafe or insulted by the things she says. All of these characteristics turn you off—at least intellectually—and you can't imagine being sexually intimate. But on another level, her body type and the way she brushes the hair off her face arouses you. You may block it on a conscious level, but your unconscious is saying you feel some desire for her that you haven't reckoned with. Do you want her or don't you? The answer is both. The dream comes to tell you what you haven't allowed into consciousness. Knowing these other layers of feelings, you will be better equipped to decide how to conduct yourself; your behavior will be more conscious.

On the other hand, perhaps the person who shows up as a sexual partner in your dream is someone you definitely don't want. You are completely clear of your lack of desire. In waking life, he doesn't turn you on in any way, and the thought of sexual contact with him might actually be repulsive. To discover why he has made an appearance in a sexual dream, we move on to the many possible metaphorical layers.

SEXUAL IMAGERY AS METAPHOR

When the literal meaning of a sexual dream does not resonate with the dreamer, then the meaning of the dream and the message it offers must be symbolic or metaphorical. Just as we use sexual language in our speech when we don't mean sex or lovemaking, we may take these expressions and turn them into literal pictures of "Screw you!" or getting screwed. We also talk about how we embrace an idea or a philosophy. In the dream, we might use a sexual or erotic image to capture this by having a particular person be the symbol for this idea or philosophy.

Again, the feeling reaction of the dreamer helps us to see whether this is embracing or screwing or some other metaphor of speech. Is it pleasant or unpleasant? Is the dreamer aroused or horrified in the dream by the activities? And how do those feelings compare with the waking emotions to these images and actions?

COMPENSATION FOR, OR MIRROR OF, WAKING STATE

A sudden increase in sexual dreams might occur for some people when their sex lives have improved or they have a new and exciting partner. An increase in sexual activity will make the subject of sex and the images more prominent in the dreamer's mind. This may be reflected in dreams. Many people say that having sex (especially after a hiatus) increases their desire for more and this, too, can show up as more sexual dreams.

On the other hand, if you're doing without sex, do not have a partner, or have an unwilling or undesirable one, your dreams might compensate for this waking lack. If you don't masturbate when your desire says you need to, then you may have sexual dreams with a partner or dreams of masturbating to satisfy this unmet urge.

ORGASMS DURING DREAMS

Both men and women report reaching orgasm in dreams. Sometimes, the dreamer will be able to reach orgasm easily and intensely in a dream compared to feeling slow or inadequate in waking life. This ease of orgasm and lack of inhibition may be another compensating effect dreams have by allowing us more freedom from our waking shame around sexuality. Many people have experienced moral condemnation or constraints around their sexual feelings and preferences and the dream allows for the expression of these feelings. In dreams, our behavior is usually outside the bounds of our waking actions, and sexual dreams are no different. When dreamers become more open and accepting of their own sexuality, they are likely to have more orgasmic dreams, regardless of their age.

The orgasm itself may also be a metaphor for a creative burst of energy with its pleasure and heightened sense of aliveness. Those feelings in the dream can spill over into creative and challenging projects in waking life. We use the metaphors of getting over the edge or making the jump when we talk about orgasms as well as leaping into creative or business ventures. Having an orgasm might symbolize getting unstuck or feeling a sense of spiritual connection with the universe. The dreamer can best say what levels of meaning this orgasm might represent beyond the purely physical release it offers.

FORBIDDEN FANTASIES

When a person has a dream of a sexual activity that she finds repugnant to her waking standards, she worries that the dream means she really wants to have this experience. Only the dreamer can know this. If you dream of masturbating in front of friends or having sex outdoors with your partner, only you know whether you'd really want to do that. Once again, we have layers of desire and aspects of our personalities that don't get a chance for expression in our daily lives. The dream affords us a place to express these fantasies, especially if our waking minds have shut them off. Betty Dodson, in her excellent book, *Sex for One: The Joy of Self-loving*, addresses the issue of giving oneself permission to have sexual fantasies.

While each of us might secretly believe our own fantasies are just too "sick" or too "kinky" to ever be revealed, there is a long list of sexual scenarios that are quite popular and harmless: playing doctor, being made to perform sexually against your will, rape scenes, sex with animals, being punished or humiliated, getting strip searched, having sex with the football team or other gang bang scenes, sex with a parent or a sibling, and even sex with angels. There is no need to pass moral judgment on our sexual imaginations. The creative mind demands a limitless field of possibilities that exists beyond the restrictions of reality and how we actually choose to experience sex. (Dodson, 1996)

What I appreciate in Betty Dodson is her joyful approach to sexuality and sensuality and her conviction that we are entitled to a rich and satisfying orgasmic life. Whatever goes on inside your head is fine and doesn't have to be feminist, compassionate, politically correct, or please your childhood religion teacher. I believe people need to make a distinction between the thought and the deed. Fantasizing about an act is not the same as doing it, nor should these thoughts or dreams cause the kind of guilt or fear you might have if you engaged in the behavior you feel is immoral or unkind to others. The dream gives an arena to ventilate and contain these imagined possibilities.

PRACTICING NEW BEHAVIORS

Sometimes, our sexual dreams are a prelude to doing the activity in the dream. Perhaps we have felt too shy or too inhibited to take an active role with a partner or to suggest a certain position. In the dream, we can ask for what we want and we get it, turning on without embarrassment or hesitation. This dream experience is a way of practicing and preparing for those things we know we want to do.

SEXUAL DREAMS ABOUT THE THERAPIST

Clients in therapy often have dreams about their therapists. The intimacy of a therapeutic relationship, especially one that may continue for an extended period of time, creates a sense of close-ness that is likely to be expressed in dreams by using sexual im-agery. The dream may express a real desire for consummation of these feelings or it may be a way of showing (in neon lights!) the familiarity the client feels toward his or her therapist. As long as the therapist (and it is the therapist's responsibility first) maintains a professional distance, allowing an expression of feelings but dis-tinguishing them from behavior, the dreamer needn't be fearful or embarrassed about these dreams. The message may be how much the dreamer has identified with the therapist, which is part of the transference process. These feelings may be turned into sexual pic-tures. Certainly, sexual dreams about your therapist should be dis-cussed as part of the therapy. A professional will hear the metaphorical layers, which might as easily be expressions of inti-macy as those of hostility (see below).

STRANGERS AND UNRECOGNIZABLE PARTNERS

In our dreams, we pick sexual partners whom we would never pick in waking life—or we think we wouldn't.

The waking mind rejects the dream's sexual behavior as *not me*. Maybe this is an aspect of our sexuality that we have not al-lowed ourselves to recognize: another part of our split-off self. Perhaps we are rehearsing a behavior we'd like to try out.

Beyond the reality that we are all more complex than we know, I once again ask the dreamer how this might be a metaphor. In what way are you embracing this person whom you wouldn't embrace in waking life. The word *embrace* is used figuratively in the language, and I want to remind the dreamer of that. Perhaps there is something about this person we admire and would like to emulate—and so we incorporate him or her, using sexual imagery as a metaphor. We might be saying that we want to be more like this person. The sexual act is one of merging, becoming one with another. It is of shared pleasure and interdependence. At its best, we feel connected in a transpersonal way with more than just our bodies. What connection does the dream express?

Or maybe it's the opposite and you are saying "Screw him!"

The details and the feelings will point the way to the dream's meaning. I ask, "How is that feeling similar to the feelings you had the day of the dream?"

For each sexual dream and each dreamer, the answers will be unique—not a formula you can look up in a book. The dreamer will have specific associations and comments about this unlikely sex partner that will also point toward the meaning of the dream.

KINKY SEX

In our dreams, there is no way to predict the kinds of sexual things we can do. Again, what we might not want to do in waking life because it is too kinky might show up in our dreams. Sometimes these sexual images are not literal representations of desire or sexual fantasy but are metaphors for other aspects of your life. If you have a dream that you are having sex with an animal, I would wonder whether this is about an identification with the characteristics you attribute to this animal. Is the animal fearless, strong, agile, swift? The sexual act might be the dreamer's desire to embody these desirable traits. If you are acting as a dominating partner in your dream or being dominated, is this more about power than sex? Or both?

Dreaming of group sex or public sex might be a desire for the literal experience, but it might also express a longing to be connected with other people in other, nonsexual ways. The sexual community in the dream might be a symbol of the passionate desire to be part of a social community in a more personal and intimate way. The sexual intimacy might be a metaphor for psychological and emotional intimacy.

Of course, whether something is kinky or not can only be decided by the individual. One person's delight is another's indignity. If you, as the dreamer, find a particular behavior too kinky to consider literally acting out, then you might want to explore the metaphorical layers of meaning this activity or this dream partner (or both) might have for you. Remember to go beyond the obvious. Explore further than first layers that come easily to mind.

TRY THIS

Think of a sexual behavior that you believe is too kinky for you to actually do. If you dreamed yourself doing it, what might you be telling yourself?

NUDITY OR EXHIBITIONISM

Dreams about being nude in public are very common, perhaps among the most common of dreams. Often the person will be out in public and discover she has no clothes on or is only partly covered. She looks around and sees no one even notices. Or perhaps everyone notices and she feels embarrassed at being naked in public and is in a hurry to get home, to hide, or cover up. These dreams are usually about public exposure. Maybe you've revealed something about yourself to others and you are concerned about how that will be received. Our language uses expressions of nudity to capture this sense of vulnerability and exposure. We say we felt naked in public when we are talking metaphorically. We talk about taking off our mask, letting our hair down, and letting it all hang out when we are referring to revealing our true selves.

Sometimes, in a dream group, participants will reveal what they consider to be a deep, dark secret. They do this with great trepidation and fear of being judged, thought crazy, or rejected.

The group members usually express surprise that this secret is such a big deal. They've been there, done that. They had those same feelings or experienced the same thing. This experience with its lack of strong reaction from the other group members might trigger a dream of being naked in public and nobody cares or notices except the dreamer.

For someone who is a nudist or is comfortable with nudity, dreams of being undressed in public might take on different meanings. Perhaps it is a desire to be more natural in other settings. Wearing clothing might symbolize being artificial or hiding one's real feelings as some nudists suggest. Clothing and accessories can be signs of the masks and props we wear to hide our insecurities and feelings of inadequacy. Clothes may also be a way to hide our fears about our bodies, how they will be desired or not desired by others, to stifle our natural sensuality.

Whether the dream is an expression of a desire to literally expose oneself sexually can only be decided by the dreamer. Do you want to strut your stuff in public? How does it feel in the dream? Is it sexy, embarrassing, or ordinary? Is exhibitionism one of your fantasies? Do you like being the center of attention or shocking others?

On the other hand, depending on how you feel in your dream of nakedness, the dream might be telling you that you've exposed yourself in some emotional way. Perhaps you are feeling too vulnerable and public and need to respect your privacy more. Maybe you need to have your boundaries more clear at work or in a personal relationship, and the distress in your dream of nakedness demands a withdrawal or cover-up from public exposure.

TRY THIS

Imagine yourself being naked in public right now. You are out somewhere alone and you look down and find you have nothing on. How does that feel? What comes to mind? What memories come up? Where are you and what does this setting mean to you?

INFIDELITY

Many people in exclusive, monogamous partnerships have dreams of their lovers being unfaithful. The image of seeing his loved one with someone else is vivid, threatening, and upsetting to the dreamer. The first question he wants to ask is whether, since dreams are so truthful, this dream is saying that his mate is cheating. This is a tough one because dreams sometimes have a literal layer of meaning. I always ask the dreamer if he has worried about this in waking life. Is there any evidence that his lover has another lover? Is this a real concern that he is not dealing with consciously?

I also ask what kind of an agreement he has or if he has assumed monogamy without an explicit agreement with the partner. Many people are so stuck in their sense of being right, of what is right (in an Absolute sense), that they can't even understand the questions. They are unable to examine this in a rational way because they feel so threatened. As in any dreamwork, this literal layer must be examined for what is real or not real with all the good sense we have in waking consciousness. The dream isn't a prophecy of future infidelity, either, unless you and your partner are on that path and the dream is reminding you of where you are going. The dreamer might ask how he is creating a situation that could lead to infidelity by how he treats his partner. Or he might want to examine how his own desires for other sexual adventures might be projected onto the partner (or someone else). The dream might then be about the dreamer's own sexual infidelity, real or fantasized.

Beyond these literal, sexual layers, the dream is often about a metaphorical infidelity. What promises have been made and are not being honored by the dreamer or others in the dreamer's life? If this were my dream, I would ask myself if I am being faithful to the vows I've made to myself to live by my principles, to take care of myself, to be fair and just and compassionate to others, to care for Mother Earth. If I have reneged on my commitments, I might portray this as a sexual infidelity. How am I cheating at something?

TRY THIS

Make a list of the promises you've made to yourself and see how many of them you haven't kept. Hint: New Year's resolutions are notorious for this kind of unfaithfulness.

HOMOSEXUAL DREAMS

Some people who identify themselves as heterosexual find sexual dreams with someone of the same gender particularly disturbing. They fear it reveals latent homosexual desires which they adamantly deny. Homosexuals are equally appalled when they dream of a sexual encounter with the opposite sex. A sexual dream with a same-sex partner doesn't make you homosexual or lesbian, nor does a heterosexual dream make you no longer gay. Only the waking dreamer can proclaim what his or her sexual orientation is. I believe the labels of homosexual, heterosexual, bisexual, or lesbian should only be self-applied. There are women who have had little or no sexual experience with other women but feel comfortable with the label of bisexual because they know their own fantasy life. Similarly, a man may have had several homosexual experiences at various times in his life, but he may think of himself only as heterosexual. The content of the dream doesn't alter this definition of the self. Only the dreamer can say whether a sexual scene in a dream is expressing a temporary or real desire rather than a metaphor of something else.

As an example, one woman in a dream workshop was concerned that her dream was saying she was lesbian. She was in her late fifties, married, and had a lifetime of exclusively heterosexual experiences. She had no conscious desire to be with a woman and wondered why her dreams would point in that direction. I asked her what a lesbian was. She said, "An independent woman, assertive, who knows her own mind, is powerful, and in charge of her own life."

The absence of a reference to anything sexual in this description was striking. I said those words back to her and she smiled, clearly hearing the way in which she wanted to embrace a lesbian.

Of course, it is possible that a dream with homosexual content is revealing to the dreamer a repressed desire or one that has not yet come to full consciousness. At the literal level, the dreamer can explore whether there is a wishful component in the sexual dream by asking about emotions and arousal in the dream. The dreamer is the final expert on whether this dream is about sex or is using sex as a metaphor to describe something else.

TRY THIS

Think of someone who is *not* a person you would choose as a sexual partner because of his or her gender or any other reason. Imagine you've just had a sexual dream about this person. Metaphorically speaking, what are you embracing, taking in, or want to be close to?

RAPE

As mentioned earlier, dreams of rape may be a metaphor for a nonsexual sense of rape. Still, I would look at the literal level first. Is there a real rape here or the possibility of one? Is my unconscious telling me I might be raped by someone or am I in some other physical danger? Am I raping myself in some way by how I'm treating my mind and body?

In current speech we talk about being violated and raped when we mean we are being treated badly, often by people who have power over us. We talk about having our privacy or our human rights violated. We also talk about raping the countryside or raping the planet. These are euphemisms, not a literal use of the terms, but our dreaming minds may turn these metaphors of speech into literal and all-too-vivid pictures.

As with all dreams, each of these layers should be looked at before we conclude we are "finished" with the dream. We may not know the full meanings of the dream until many months after the dream. And there are layers that may remain unknown for years.

TRY THIS

Metaphorically speaking, who has raped or violated you in your life? Conversely, what or whom have you raped?

SEX AND VIOLENCE

As with dreams of rape, when sex and violence are linked in dreams, it is important for the dreamer to ask what literal threat the dream may be warning the dreamer about. Are those who are violent in the dream acting as they do in waking life or are they behaving out of character? Are they known or unknown? Are the violent characters behaving in some violent way toward the dreamer? Perhaps the dream is a more vivid depiction of the waking character who is perpetrating emotional violence if not physical violence in waking life.

INCEST

Dreams of incest are often very disturbing and nightmarish for the dreamer. In particular, a dream of sex with a family member who is a child will so offend the dreamer that she might not want to tell the dream to someone else, fearing she has turned into a pedophile and a degenerate. As with any dream, if the literal content does not seem to have meaning for the dreamer, a metaphorical or symbolic layer will usually disclose the insight. What are the characteristics of this partner and how might you want to embrace them, incorporate them as part of yourself? If the sexual partner is a child, perhaps you are trying to restore in yourself the hope and joyfulness of a child. How does what you are doing feel? Like affection or violation?

If you are on the receiving end of an incestuous encounter in your dreams, does this feel more like sexual play or like violence? As with any dreams, your perception and emotions around the events in the dream will help reveal the dream's meanings.

REPRESSED MEMORIES

For the last several years, it has been in vogue to find sexual abuse in nearly everyone's childhood. Certainly sexual abuse exists and probably is more common than most people have recognized or want to believe. However, a broad range of symptoms common to most people have been listed as evidence of incest and sexual violation (Bass & Davis, 1988). Dreams and nightmares have come to be considered by some to be a reliable source of memories. In particular, people look to dreams as proof of sexual experiences and traumas that have been repressed by the conscious mind. Taking any dream solely at a literal level is a misunderstanding of how both dreams and memory work, as was discussed briefly in chapter 1, and a further exploration of this debate is beyond the scope of this book. But, as with all dreams, I caution dreamers to use their waking, critical minds to determine what in a dream is a true and accurate replay of some literal event and what is not. A dream is a distortion of any true facts and is told in symbolic language. Dreams of abduction, rape, and molestation by family members are more likely to be metaphors for other kinds of violation, as we have discussed throughout this chapter. Acceptance of these images as literal depictions of past events or memories of real events can be dangerous. Accepting the belief that these events really happened can cause more trauma than any historical event may have. (See Loftus and Ketchum [1991, 1994], Yapko [1994], and Ofshe and Watters [1994].) James Hillman said it well in *We've Had a Hundred Years of Psychotherapy and the World's Getting Worse:*

I'm not saying children aren't molested or abused. They *are* molested, and they *are* abused, and in many cases it's absolutely devastating. But therapy makes it even more devastating *by the way it thinks about it*. It isn't just the trauma that does the damage; it's remembering traumatically. (Hillman and Ventura, 1992, p. 25. Emphasis in the original.)

LAYERS OF MEANING

As with all dreams, it is important to see both the subject and object levels of the dream characters. In what way do these characters represent real people in your life and the way they are treating you? And then ask how these characters are parts of you projected outward onto others or strangers. An *aha* on one level doesn't preclude an *aha* on another. There are usually meanings on both the subject and object levels.

GETTING BACK INTO THE DREAM

Many people ask whether it is possible to get back into a dream if they've been awakened before the dream is over. Often, they ask this question while referring to pleasant dreams they want to return to. More often these are dreams with erotic content and imagery and they would like to finish this one—perhaps with an orgasm.

In general, some people can return to a dream at will. When I speak to large groups, I often ask how many can do this. About half of my audiences (which may be a self-selected sample and not representative of the general population) say they can return to a dream. They are able to get up and use the bathroom or get a drink of water, return to bed, and pick up the dream where it left off. The other half of the people say they can't do this, even when they want to, and will start a whole new dream. Perhaps this is a difference in the way people approach tasks with some being able to return when distracted and others beginning a whole new train of thought. I am in the latter category. Instead of returning to a dream, I'm likely to start a new one. The dreams will have some relationship, but my imagery and the story will be a new metaphor for the same subject.

If you want to return to a dream, here are a few techniques that work for some people. Some of these are a review of those discussed in chapter 5.

1. Return to the sleep position you were in when you woke up. If you can't remember, return to your favorite and most frequent sleep position.

2. Try to recapture the feelings and sensations you were having in the dream when you woke up.

3. Whatever you remember of the dream, replay the events and setting in your mind, attempting to reenter it as closely as possible.

4. Tell yourself you're going back to the dreamscape.

5. Expect to return to this dream as if this is something you regularly do. (Expectation has a strong influence on outcome.)

6. Imagine yourself standing and spinning, turning around and around as you reenter the dream.

If you have trouble getting back into the dream, pretend you have. Use your imagination and fantasy to be wherever you want to be and to finish the dream as you like.

·*nine*·

Common Dreams
and Themes

❧

THERE ARE MANY COMMON DREAMS THAT people have throughout the world. Some of these universal symbols appear in all cultures, regardless of the available technology or belief system. Jung explored many of these archetypes, as he called them, at length. Some universal symbols are images of the good mother, the wise old person, the trickster, the innocent child. When working with such universal figures and metaphors, it is especially important not to rely solely on what others have written about these images. Remember, it's your own reaction and interpretation of these symbols that matters.

When doing dreamwork with common dreams, it is important not to get caught up in any kind of dreamwork dogma or psychological models. What fits well for one dreamer may be alien to another. The dreamer is the only person who can elucidate the meaning of a symbol, even a universal one, because she will use it in a personal and idiosyncratic way. The particular description, the emotions of the dreamer, and the personal associations of the dreamer are the only reliable pointers to meaning.

What I present in the exploration of common dreams in this chapter are simply suggestions for working with these images. At no time do I mean to imply that these are the meanings of these dreams or the only possible ways of approaching this imagery.

Also, when looking at a literal layer of meaning of a dream, finding a meaning that resonates doesn't rule out the possibility that your unconscious also used this image for a metaphorical layer of meaning, perhaps more than one. Don't stop at your first *aha*. With any dream, you are likely to find several possible layers of meaning if you take the time to look for them.

HOUSES AND OTHER STRUCTURES

Dreams about houses are usually a metaphor for the dreamer rather than a literal statement about any particular house. A common one is finding more rooms in the house or apartment where you live. The dreamer walks through her home and discovers there are extra bedrooms, bathrooms, huge spaces she didn't know about before. These may be furnished with antiques and other valuables, or contain clothing of ornate and unusual descriptions. Or there are elegant parties in these newly discovered rooms, populated with interesting and eccentric people. The dreamer usually is delighted. "Wow!" she says. "I never knew this was here and it's wonderful!" In these dreams of finding extra space, the dreamer is usually very pleased.

This is an extremely common dream that people delight in having and telling. It's a sort of dream-version of winning the lottery. We have these dreams at times when we venture into new areas, when our lives open up. Sometimes these dreams come as the result of being in therapy or after a period of intense spiritual practice. The house is a common representation for the self or the body and this is a positive statement about our expanded self-image. We discover there is more to us than we thought, and we are awed and pleased.

At other times, the dreams of houses may be less than pleasant. There may be rooms the dreamer is afraid to enter knowing there is something dangerous waiting to leap out. This may represent the dreamer's sense of his psyche or unconscious where he fears there are things he is unwilling to face about himself. Doing inner work means we find out about our defects of character, or our dark side with unbridled rage and without moral compunctions. For some people this is frightening and the dream images say, "I don't want to go there."

If the dreamer sees a house at a distance and it is dilapidated or falling apart, I would ask the dreamer how this represents him. It might be a warning about his physical health, which he has neglected for too long. (See "Health of the Body, Body Parts," p. 148.) Or it may represent his emotional or mental status. Perhaps the dreamer feels he's falling down (on the job?) or falling apart (on the verge of a breakdown?). If the house is breaking apart, I'd listen to how this dreamer uses this metaphor in speech, perhaps to refer to a relationship breaking up.

Dreams of houses with leaky roofs or cracked foundations might have a literal layer for the dreamer, especially in the older populations who worry about the physical frailties that come with aging. With each form the images take, we want to explore the specifics with the dreamer to see exactly what the message might be.

Houses under construction are common dream images for people who are doing personal growth work. Again, these images come up for people who are making major life changes, in transition or psychotherapy, or who are overhauling their personalities and worldview through a spiritual practice. Perhaps they feel they are rebuilding themselves. I would ask about the plans, problems, and methods for the reconstruction in the dream and see how these may be metaphors for how the dreamer is feeling and viewing the project on the self. Does the dreamer have blueprints? If so, who designed them? Are they subject to revision as the plans are made? Who is in charge of the reconstruction site? All these answers will point the way to understanding who the dreamer feels is in charge and who is planning the dreamer's future. Is it the dreamer or some outside force or authority?

TRY THIS

Imagine you have a dream about building a new house for yourself. See the house before you, in progress but not yet finished. What details do you discern about the building? What is complete, what not complete? What is it made of? Do you see this in color? Who made these specific choices? Are you pleased with them? After you record this image of your house, ask yourself how your details represent how you see yourself. Remember this is a waking imagination and you may "color it" to suit your image of yourself, unlike the more honest picture you would likely get in a dream.

HEALTH OF THE BODY, BODY PARTS

When you dream specifically about your health or a particular part of your body, it is very important to investigate the literal layer of meaning of this kind of dream. In fact, all dreams should be checked out on this layer in case your unconscious is aware of a physical disease process or illness before you are aware of it consciously. In house dreams, finding a room with something gross or smelly, especially in the dark recesses of the house, might refer to some disease process in the body. The dreamer will feel a sharp tingle of resonance if there is truth in this suggestion. If the dreamer is uncertain or if the dream persists, it is certainly best to see a physician and determine if there is a physical basis for a problem as depicted in the dream. Rotten fruit and moldy purses are images that have shown up in the dreams of women with diseases or a dysfunction of their reproductive organs. Of course, these might also be metaphors for the deteriorating state of their sexual relationships, but the dreamer should be able to see what fits and what doesn't for them, their experiences, and their lives.

Many other dreams may represent the health of the body in some way. Finding your car has been demolished on one side, that part of your desk is missing, or even seeing broken limbs on trees and shrubbery may be metaphors for the body. Explore this layer with most if not all your dreams. (See step 12 of 20 Steps for Dreamwork in the Appendices.)

TEETH

In chapter 4, we discussed the possible layers of meanings for dreams about losing teeth or teeth crumbling. This is a fairly common dream, regularly reported in dream groups. (See chapter 4, under the heading: Literal Meanings First.)

TRY THIS

If all your teeth fell out, how would you feel? What would be your greatest concerns? What would you do about it? How does this reflect your feelings about yourself, your appearance, your sense of competence?

SCHOOL DREAMS

School dreams are common, especially for those who were concerned about their academic achievement and higher education. Dreams set in school or college will persist in adults many years after the person has completed his formal education. Even those with advanced degrees will find themselves in high school or undergraduate school with the usual dream dilemmas found in school dreams.

UNPREPARED FOR TEST, FINAL EXAM

In many dreams, the dreamer finds herself back in school. She knows she has to take a test, perhaps a final exam, yet she is completely unprepared. She's never gone to class for the entire semester, she has no notebook to study from, or she's lost her notes. The overall feeling is one of being unprepared, worried, and anxious. Sometimes, this is a class one needs to complete a degree and the dreamer is baffled that she has been so negligent and now will not graduate as planned. In its most extreme form, the dreamer is terrified about this, feeling as if she has overlooked something important and this will impact heavily on her future career or educational aspirations.

I have heard this dream from people who successfully completed their law degrees or Ph.D.s as many as thirty years ago. Yet the dream will show up occasionally, puzzling the dreamer. Why now? they wonder. That's a good place to begin the questioning. Clearly, if you've completed school, you're not worried about taking a real test. So I ask the dreamer in what way he feels he is being tested. If the fear and worry in the dream is particularly strong, I want to know what is happening in the person's life right now that feels like a test. In what way is he feeling unprepared? And what might be a disaster if he has not properly prepared for something? This may be a test of his honesty, his integrity, or his moral fiber. It may be about having to give a presentation at work or the expectation of a job interview or promotion. Do you have the feeling someone is testing you or are you testing someone else, in a love relationship, perhaps, or in a friendship where you are testing loyalty or honesty?

TRY THIS

In your personal/dream journal, make some notes to the following questions: At this time of your life, in what way are you being tested? How are you unprepared for the tests in your life today? How do you test others (their loyalty, honesty, trustworthiness)?

FORGETTING YOUR LINES

For other people, the test dreams above may take the form of having to give a speech or be in a school play and you've forgotten your lines. The panic sets in and you are horrified at the realization that you have no idea what to say next and, in fact, have probably never studied the script for this performance. As above, ask yourself how you are feeling unprepared for some presentation. Perhaps you feel you should give a speech to someone by telling him or her what you feel or what is troubling you. You might want to express positive sentiments toward someone and plan to say so, but you're afraid you'll lose your words.

On the other hand, "having lines" might have other connotations. A man who forgets his line might be changing his methods for attracting women and this change can be positive. "A line" usually has the underlying implication of being insincere or devious. Or perhaps this refers to lines of communication in business. Lines might also refer to cocaine use. What does the dreamer say about this phrase and how are these terms used in the dreamer's speech?

TRY THIS

Imagine you've forgotten your lines in a dream. What have you neglected to say in life that you should have said? What do you need to say to those around you to speak your truth? Do a journal entry to express your personal truths. Let it all out!

CAN'T FIND YOUR CLASSROOM

Another variation of the school dreams above, this one contains shades of feeling out of place or lost. Of course, we ask the dreamer how this feels. Have you been to this class before? Why do you need to go? Has the class been moved or have you forgotten where you were supposed to be? Each of these might reflect a particular emotional state for the dreamer. Many of us are on a lifelong quest of learning and growing. It's possible that not being able to find your classroom reflects the confusion in this quest until one settles into a path of study and growth—at least until the next period of confusion comes up again at the next plateau.

LOST YOUR CLASS SCHEDULE

This is similar to the one above. Many times, the dreamer is back in school and can't find his schedule of classes. Where is he supposed to be and how will he find out? If he can't remember what class he's supposed to be attending, how can he ask where it is? As the dream proceeds, the dreamer is increasingly anxious about being late even if he does get to class.

Looking at this dream as a metaphor about your life, you might ask what you have enrolled in (for your life's work, seeing your life's journey as a kind of class) and have not shown up for or completed the course work for. In other words, you have chosen a life mission but are telling yourself you are not accomplishing that mission.

As with all these variations on a theme, it is important to explore with the dreamer the feelings in the dream. What did it feel like? What did you understand as the problem and what might be the consequences? My version of this dream reflects my need to have a clear schedule and to be on time for the things I need to do. I hate to be late or unprepared or feel lost. If I have this dream, it's usually about feeling as though I'm doing too much and so neglecting the details in some way. I am risking either doing the task poorly or not getting it done at all. Maybe I've overscheduled myself and I'm having trouble keeping track of everything. Time to slow down. What might it mean for you? Remember! Your mileage may vary.

BATHROOMS, TOILETS

When I began dreamwork with the public, I was surprised at the number of dreams people have about bathrooms. Dreamers are sometimes reluctant to share these dreams because they find them vulgar or embarrassing. Our cultural norms still discourage detailed discussion of body processes unless we use the most technical and clinical terms. This, of course, is the antithesis of the spirit of good dreamwork where we let it all hang out.

Most dreamers interpret bathroom dreams to be telling them that they really had to go to the bathroom while they were sleeping. Indeed, they got up and went to the toilet. Commonly, this urge will trigger the imagery of the dream. For most people trying to understand their dreams, this is where they will stop—at the literal interpretation of the dream. I say, "Okay. That's layer one." What else might this dream be saying by using this particular metaphor?

In some variations of this dream, the dreamer has to go to the bathroom but can't find one. The toilets may all be occupied or they are too dirty to use. The dream generally takes place in a public space. Perhaps the stalls are pay toilets and the dreamer doesn't have the needed change. Often the toilet is not private or what first looked to be a private place is not. Maybe there is a clear window behind the dreamer or there is an audience of people who have full view of the toilet and the dreamer's actions. The dreamer might know he's being watched though not have a clear explanation of how he knows this. Or he might be more concerned that people can hear what he's doing and this is embarrassing or humiliating. Possibly, the dreamer feels enraged at being intruded upon during this private function. Sometimes women dream of men barging into the ladies' bathroom in a public facility.

In each case, we want the dreamer to express the feelings and thoughts in the dream. How is this dream an expression of the thoughts and feelings about something in the dreamer's waking life? *This is the question to ask of any dream.*

In my experience of examining dreams about bathrooms and toilets, the dreamer is often indicating a need to express some thoughts or feelings in waking life but has been unable to find a suitable place. To let it all out or have "diarrhea of the mouth" as some call it, you have to have a safe place, a place that feels private enough to do your business.

As you can hear, these toilet metaphors are part of our speech when we talk about someone who wants to share his or her innermost feelings. For many, these hidden feelings are as private as their excretory functions. This is echoed in the toilet habits of some people who can't move their bowels when they are on vacation or in public toilets. They feel constricted in strange or public places. Is the dreamer feeling constipated? We use this word as a description for people who are uptight, stiff, and hold their feelings in.

When someone reports a bathroom dream, I want to know what particular feelings come up for the individual dreamer. Is there repulsion at the messes of others in these dirty toilets? Perhaps this is the dreamer's aversion to listening to other people's shit. Might the disgust be about one's own excrement and having a place to let go of it? If you don't have money for a pay toilet, this might be about feeling you have to pay to find a place where you can safely let your shit out, as in therapy or other professional help. Perhaps in your dream group or therapy group you are having some anxiety about revealing personal details of yourself, and this feels like having to use a bathroom without the privacy you expect.

TRY THIS

Imagine you have had a dream of being in a bathroom in a public building. What happens? How do you feel? How is this a statement about revealing yourself and your inner processes? What does this tell you about yourself right now?

FLYING

Many people have flying dreams at various times of their lives. In this dream, they are flying unassisted, without a plane or wings. Some fly vertically, zooming along with their feet off the ground. Others fly like Superman with arms outstretched like wings. Usually, the feelings attached to this dream experience are positive. The dreamer feels happy, exhilarated, free, and strong. These dreams often come when the dreamer is feeling good about herself. She is feeling competent and able to do things she has never done before.

The image of flying is sometimes a literal picture of our metaphor of saying we're really flying when things are going well. We might say we're soaring or floating on a cloud. What words do you use to express that you're feeling your best? These might show up as flying images in your speech and in your dreams.

(*Note: I have a personal theory that the frequency of this type of flying dream could be correlated with other measures of self-esteem, but I don't believe such a study has ever been done.)

Sometimes, flying above others might echo your feelings of superiority, and the dream is calling you on this arrogance. Of course, there are times when feeling you are above it all is an excellent way to cope with the petty vexations of everyday life.

For some people, flying in a dream carries some anxiety. They are flying out of something or away from something. I ask what they might be trying to escape in their waking life, so much so that they wish they could just fly away. Or in the dream, they are worried about whether they can really fly and they are afraid they will crash. Perhaps they have suddenly been elevated in some way (with a promotion on the job or getting public recognition for their courage), and they don't know if they can keep it up. The last phrase might also have a sexual connotation. For some people, the imagery and pleasure of flying are related to sexual ecstasy.

TRY THIS

Make up a flying dream. Where do you fly to? How does it feel? What does this tell you about how you feel about yourself?

FALLING

Falling dreams are extremely common. In any audience I speak to, more than half say they have had dreams of falling. The dream is usually accompanied by a physical sensation of falling. This might be frightening enough that the dreamer wakes with a start in the middle of the fall or sometimes at the moment of impact. Customarily, these dreams come at the time of drifting off to sleep. One explanation is that the dream is a representation of the mental awareness of the sensation of falling asleep. And observe our language: we say falling asleep. We also use the terms dropping off to sleep or slipping into sleep, each using metaphors of falling or loss of bodily control in some way. This is, of course, accurate; we go inward and our minds are more active when we're sleeping, while our bodies seem to drop away from our conscious awareness. Physiologically, entering sleep must feel like falling.

In addition to the literal layer, I would explore the metaphorical layer of falling for the dreamer. Have you fallen off the wagon? Fallen from grace? Are you a fallen woman? Did you fall in love? A fallen soldier is a euphemism for one who has died. If the dreamer is British, the term might be used by a woman who, when saying she fell, might be using the colloquial term for getting pregnant.

If the dreamer seems to take the fall willingly or passively, I would explore the expressions of being the fall guy, which refers to taking the blame for something that someone else is responsible for. Another possibility is that the dreamer has fallen for something (or someone) and thereby been deceived. I would proceed to look for other themes of deception or being captivated without critical scrutiny. What way did you fall in the day before the dream?

There are so many uses for the word *fall* that I would encourage the dreamer to see the many dictionary definitions to help arrive at one or two meanings that feel correct for him or her. The dreamer should remember to explore what comes to mind at the words *fall* or *falling* and what the feelings were in the dream. At different times in one's life, the image and sensation of falling will hold different meanings. Each dream will have a current and practical meaning for the dreamer.

FINDING MONEY, TREASURES, JEWELS (OR FAMILY JEWELS)

One of the most pleasant common dreams is one of finding money. Perhaps the dreamer is walking down the street and picking up money, stuffing it into his pockets. Or the dreamer comes upon an unexpected treasure. He might think, Should I keep it? How much is it worth? The treasure could be gold coins, paper money in a trunk, ancient and valuable documents, a manuscript, or jewelry. What kind of treasure is this? The dreamer's associations to the particular treasure would help toward understanding its meaning. The form a treasure takes and the thoughts the dreamer has about it are very important. A stamp collection would make me think of my father, but cut crystal would call up images of my mother.

I would ask the dreamer how he felt upon finding this treasure. This could be a delightful bonanza or the beginning of a problem, as winning the lottery has turned out to be for some people. If the feelings are mostly positive and hopeful, I would ask how this reflects how the dreamer feels about someone in his life. Is she a real treasure? Or perhaps this represents a treasure the dreamer has discovered in himself. What treasures inside of you (talents, skills, strengths, capabilities, creative gold mines) have you just come in contact with? Clients in psychotherapy or on other kinds of personal growth journeys will have this dream when they discover they have value as they are, there is more to them than they thought, and they feel good about themselves as human beings. The dream could be saying that you feel you are a treasure to yourself.

If the jewels the dreamer finds are a family heirloom, consider the expressions about family jewels, often referring to a man's testicles. If a woman finds the family jewels, might she be feeling as if she now has balls? That is, how is she more powerful and what we think of as manly?

LOSING YOUR PURSE, WALLET, KEYS

Women frequently dream of losing their purses while men dream of losing their wallets. Both men and women dream of losing their keys, briefcases, or important documents. Such dreams, while possibly having a literal layer of warning to be more careful with these valuables, more often express the dreamer's anxiety over a loss of power or identity. For most of us, what we carry in a purse or wallet is very important: personal identification, driver's license, credit cards, keys, money, social security card, insurance information, health information, perhaps a phone book, photos, or a treasured item. What would the loss of all these items mean to the dreamer? And what might the consequences be? What is important in arriving at meaning is how the dreamer interprets this loss. One dreamer might focus on not being able to get into his house, another on the financial problems of money lost. Someone else might have something in a wallet or purse that is secret, and having others find it could be problematic or precipitate an encounter with legal authorities. What does the dreamer think of when he or she realizes what is lost? What does the dreamer do in the dream to resolve the problem? All these will point the way to what meaning this dream has at the time of the dream. This might not always be the same each time the dream occurs, even if it is a recurrent dream. The issues of identity and security might be financial at one time and relate to fears of loss of identity in a relationship at another time.

GETTING LOST

Dreams of being in a strange place and feeling lost or dreams of losing one's way usually come at a time when the dreamer is feeling lost in some way in his waking life. Are you lost in the shuffle? Have you lost your direction for a particular path you have chosen? If you felt clear about your future at one time but now feel as if you are without direction, you might have dreams of being lost. Perhaps the scenery seems familiar and you believe you should know the way, but you are still lost. How does this represent how you feel in waking life? Your feeling lost might refer to one or more areas of your life—intellectually or in terms of your career path, spiritually, or in your love relationships. If this is a recurrent dream, I would want to examine along with the dreamer how she feels her life has been in confusion or how it has been aimless. As I ask with all recurrent dreams, *When did this dream begin and what happened at the time of the onset of this dream theme?*

LOSING YOUR CAR OR YOUR CAR IS STOLEN (OR LOSING OTHER VALUABLE ITEMS)

For those of us who drive a car in metropolitan areas, losing our car is not an uncommon event. Where did I park the car? Did I go out the wrong door of the mall so I am now in a different parking lot? This is something I've done, and so it shows up occasionally in my dreams as a metaphor. I also once had a car stolen.

I left the house to go to work and discovered my car was gone. This image with its strong emotions left its mark, sometimes showing up in my dreams years later.

Layer one is the literal layer. Are you at risk of losing your car in some way, perhaps to the loan company for not making your payments? Are you taking a risk by your choice of where you're parking your car so it could be towed away or stolen?

For many of us, cars and having our own car means having freedom to go where we want when we want. The car has become a modern symbol of autonomy and independence. If your car is lost or stolen in a dream, you might want to see how you resolve the dilemma in the dream. Do you call a taxi? Do you call your parents or spouse to pick you up? The dream might be saying something about how you feel you have lost your freedom and not having wheels might represent it well. How the dreamer resolves the problem in the dream will help point the way to possible meanings.

CAR ACCIDENTS OR CARS OUT OF CONTROL, DRIVING

Dreams about car accidents or cars out of control often worry people. They fear the dream may be a warning of an impending accident in waking life, or that they will lose control of their car due to some mechanical defect or their improper handling.

As with most dreams, this is usually a metaphor rather than a prophecy of a literal event happening or an image of events happening to others at a distance.

If you dream of having a car accident or your car is out of control, begin by asking yourself how this describes your present state. Are you about to have a crash? Is it financial, emotional, or relating to some other aspect of your life? Might you be moving toward a health crisis because you aren't taking care of yourself? The crash might represent a personal financial disaster you are about to face but are only aware of unconsciously as yet. Who is having the crash in the dream? Is this person you or is it someone who represents a part of you?

If the car is out of control and you are the one driving, examine how this might describe the way you're running your life. Do you have brakes or are you unable to stop the car's movement in the dream? Perhaps the dream is telling you that you feel you are unable to stop yourself from doing something in waking life that could be dangerous or lethal.

Are you driving the car, or is someone else at the wheel? Perhaps this is another of our metaphors of speech made literal by the dream. If you are not driving the car, try asking yourself who is in the driver's seat in your life. Whoever is driving the car in the dream is the one in control. The driver is the one who decides where the car goes and how to get to your destination. Is this the person you want to be in power? The dream could be telling you that you are not empowered in your own life or that you have given up control to someone else. It is interesting to note that I know of one woman who has never driven a car in waking life due to a physical disability, yet she is the one driving in her dreams. She believes this is clearly a statement of how she feels herself to be self-empowered; she is the one in charge of her own life.

PLANES, TRAINS, BOAT CRASHES

Similarly, dreams about crashes of other vehicles such as trains, boats, and planes might be symbols for the crash course we feel we are on. We say someone is an accident waiting to happen, and sometimes the dream will give us this evaluation in pictures of major accidents. If we are about to take a trip on one of these vehicles, the crash may capture our ambivalence about going or our fears about travel. In each case, look at what happens in your dream and how you feel about these events. Do you take action in the dream to save yourself or others? Or are you a passive victim? How is this a statement about your journey through life?

SWIMMING, DROWNING

Whether you are a competent swimmer or not, you might dream about having difficulty swimming or have images of drowning. The literal layer could be a warning to be more careful in circumstances involving water. Perhaps you have become overly confident or are taking unnecessary risks.

On the metaphorical level, I want to ask the dreamer what he's drowning in. Bills? Paperwork? Deadlines? Laundry? Is this a familiar dream or a familiar theme for the dreamer? Drowning is a common symbol used for feeling overwhelmed or stressed by life's demands. You might be saying to yourself that you can't keep your head above water or that you're in over your head. Do you know how to swim in the dream or not? Do you feel you can overcome this dilemma or are you feeling powerless and exhausted? These feelings will come from your waking feelings and experiences.

WATER

Many times people have approached me and asked, "I dream about water. What does it mean?" Dreams of water are common because water is a constant part of our daily life, but also because water is used as a universal symbol of important life issues. In religious traditions, water has been referred to in the water of life, baptism, and the cleansing of sin. There is the *mikvah,* a bathing ritual among Orthodox Jewish women. Water is a universal symbol of fertility, growth, new life, and creative potential. Water is often described as feminine in origin, especially in Asian culture where it is considered to be yin. Water may also be a symbol of the unconscious, especially if the dreamer is preoccupied with its being deep or dark and is concerned with probing its depths. People involved in psychotherapy or psychoanalysis might dream of diving into deep waters as they explore the unknown depths of their psyche, generally with some fear and trepidation as well as curiosity and a longing to explore.

If you have a dream with water in it, and it's likely that you will, you will want to notice what the water is like. Is it dark, foul, deep, or shallow? How do you describe it? The description will usually reveal the emotional component of this symbol. And then, how does this relate to your waking life? Certainly, if you just had a hot tub installed in your home, water will have a certain set of associations. Compare that to how you might feel about water if you've just been through a flood or major hurricane. If you are a woman about to have a baby, water will mean something else. This symbol may be used in different ways with different meanings for individual dreamers at different times of their lives.

BEING CHASED

Have you dreamed of someone chasing you? A monster or demon? An animal or scary person? Perhaps you knew you were being chased, but you didn't know who or what it was that was chasing you.

For many dreamers, this is a terrifying dream and sometimes a recurrent theme. If there is no one in the dreamer's life who is literally in pursuit, such as a stalker, I would ask if there is a suitor in waking life. Does someone want a relationship and is chasing the dreamer out of admiration and desire? If none of these resonates, then we move to the other layers of the dream. Perhaps this is an image of other kinds of feeling chased. Are you feeling chased by bill collectors or the IRS? Do you have an uncompleted project or deadline that you feel is chasing you?

The specifics of who or what is doing the chasing and how the dreamer reacts will reveal what the dream's message is. If the one in pursuit is an animal or a monster, a description of how the dreamer feels toward this being will help to make a bridge to the waking concerns the dreamer is expressing through this dream.

Certainly, being chased by a grizzly bear rather than a little puppy would carry different meanings.

The temptation for many dreamers with this common dream is to "explain" its occurrence by saying it came on the heels of a scary movie or watching the evening news before bedtime. I respond, "Okay. That's layer one." Now we can explore why you snatched the image of the man with a gun chasing someone in the movie to use it in your dream about yourself. Who is chasing you with a gun? What is the gun—a work project? a boss? a family member? And in what way are you holding a gun to your own head by making demands on yourself that are unreasonable and more stressful than they need to be?

If we remember to see each person in the dream as a part of ourselves, then we are the scary killer, the demon, or the monster. This Shadow layer of the dream is often the most difficult to see because it is denied and disowned. You might want to review the concept of the Shadow in chapter 8 as it applies to dreams of being chased. Also, recall the woman who kept saying she was always chased in her dreams. Because she kept saying it the same way, never saying someone was chasing her or pursuing her, I wrote out the word *chaste* for her. She had an immediate *aha* of recognition. Remember to look for plays on words and puns in your exploration of your choice of dream images.

FEELING PARALYZED, UNABLE TO SCREAM

Sometimes in a dream, we are trying to scream for help, or trying to run away from something, and we can't do either. No sound comes out. Our feet won't move at all, or we feel we are stuck in slow motion. This sleep paralysis is a natural event caused by the release of chemicals in the brain during REM sleep, which prevents us from acting out our dream. These short-lived chemicals literally paralyze our voluntary muscles, preventing us from physically carrying out actions that could be harmful to ourselves or our sleep partners. But our awareness of this paralysis sometimes adds to the nightmarish quality of the dream. A few moments later, these chemicals are metabolized and we can move again.

Some people experience a short delay in this coming to full wakefulness and may feel as if they are awake or half awake and are literally paralyzed. The experience can be very frightening and may include visions or hallucinations of people in the room or physical threats. But these apparitions and the paralysis will dissipate in a few minutes as the person returns to full wakefulness.

At the metaphorical layer, ask yourself how you might be paralyzed in life. Are you feeling stuck? Are you having trouble taking some action you've been putting off? Are you unable to speak up when you need to? Is it time to do some shouting about something or someone?

DEATH AND DYING

Because so many people have the mistaken belief that all dreams are prophecies of the future, dreams about death can be especially frightening. Another mistaken belief is that if we dream something, it is what we wish to happen, so a dream about death might be falsely translated to mean we wish to die or we are wishing death on someone else. The dreamer will know if there is any truth here, and any interpretations from others can only be projections of their own feelings and their own situations.

The literal layer of meaning has relevance for the dreamer in terms of an impending death of someone when there is already a concern about this happening. Getting close to someone might trigger fears of loss, expressed in a dream of losing the loved one. This is especially true for those who have had a lot of losses in life. A person who has lost one or both parents early in life or suddenly lost a lover or mate to a tragedy might fear this happening again. He might have dreams expressing the fear of this loss when another relationship promises closeness and security.

However, dreams about death are more frequently a metaphor describing a major change or transformation in the dreamer's life. You are likely to dream about death during periods of big transitions in life. When you graduate from school to enter the working world, a part of you must die for you to move on to the next stage. The little child must die to dependency, emotional outburst, and irresponsibility for the adult to emerge and function competently and responsibly.

Who is dying in the dream? How do you, as the dreamer, react to this knowledge? Are you trying to save this person or are you resigned to this death being inevitable? Do you grieve or feel relief? You might want to see how the death of this person represents a part of yourself that must die at this stage of your life. A divorce is a death of a marriage, but for many people it is a positive new beginning and comes with a feeling of release and peace.

Perhaps the death in the dream symbolizes a part of yourself you need to kill off: the one who is holding you back from progress, who discourages you and limits you, the part of you who entices you to make unhealthy life choices. A death of that part of you will liberate you to do your life's work, to be more productive and satisfied. If you are dreaming about the death of your mother, who is still living, for example, you might ask yourself how the part of you that is like your mother needs to die.

Note: If you are dreaming of suicide and have conscious thoughts about making a plan to kill yourself, see a mental-health professional at once! Suicide is a permanent solution to a temporary problem. This hard time will pass and you may look back on this difficult period as the one that propelled you into the best times of your life.

On the other hand, dreams about suicide might be less than literal. The dream might be saying you are killing yourself by the way you are living: by your poor health or eating habits, by overwork, by not nurturing yourself through the stresses of life. What's killing you and how are you doing this to yourself? You might blame your job, but the question is why you've made the choice to stay there and have a living death.

If you dream about jumping off a cliff, does this feel deadly or exhilarating? Are you taking the plunge in some positive way or do you feel this represents a suicidal or catastrophic leap?

Any dream that feels like a warning to the dreamer should be taken seriously. After working with my dreams for many years, I know my dreaming of the death of someone else is likely to be about me or a part of myself. I symbolize this aspect of myself by the figure of this other person. Still, I would not hesitate to tell someone I dreamed of her death. Maybe, on another level, I am concerned for her safety and the consequences of her recklessness. A discussion with this person may bring us to a new stage of friendship and intimacy and an understanding of each other as well as ourselves.

DECEASED PERSONS IN DREAMS

Sometimes we will dream about dead relatives and friends, some of them dead for decades. Some people will wonder how this dream can be a current issue when these deceased people haven't been in the dreamer's life for such a long time. Dreams are always current as well as historical, just as we think about the past when we are having our waking experiences in the present. We compare them, note the similarities and the differences. Sometimes people in our present remind us of people who are no longer in our lives and we will symbolize these present individuals with figures from our past. Perhaps a man I met reminds me of my father. Or the woman I had lunch with said exactly the kinds of things my mother would have said to me. ("You would look so much better if your hair were short!") These events call up memories of people from the past who then show up in our dreams. The memory might not be fully conscious, but at a feeling level, we are thrown back into another time.

If people from the past are present in your dream, what is happening now that reminds you of this person? How is someone in your life today treating you in the same way as this past person did? Are the feelings positive or negative? Would you like to have another person like the deceased one in your life again? Is your life in a comparable place to the time represented by the person in the dream?

At another level, does this deceased person represent a part of you? It is a basic psychological principle that we incorporate the beliefs, habits, prejudices, and worldview of our parents, whether we want to or not. This is also true of our extended family (aunts, uncles, grandparents) if we had a lot of exposure to them.

Some people spend much of their lives undoing the indoctrination of their family of origin. Your dream of an argument with a deceased family member may be expressing your inner conflict with the part of you that has absorbed the traits or beliefs of this person.

NAKED IN PUBLIC

Dreams of being naked in public are usually about feelings of being exposed and being vulnerable. Frequently, the dreamer is naked and no one seems to notice or care, though the dreamer is trying desperately to cover up or find her clothing. See chapter 8 for a more complete discussion of dreams of nudity and exhibitionism in dreams.

NATURAL DISASTERS: TORNADOES, TIDAL WAVES, FIRES, HURRICANES, FLOODS, EARTHQUAKES, LIGHTNING, VOLCANOES

Dreams will sometimes contain images of natural disasters. The particular choice of disaster is probably influenced by your experience and fears, what geographical area you live in or have lived in before, and the images left over from your day (what Freud referred to as "day residues") such as hearing news reports, reading, or movies. Living in South Florida, I have had a few hurricane scares and no exposure to earthquakes. I am probably more likely to dream about the former than the latter, though I have also dreamed of fires and tornadoes and haven't had experience with either.

Disaster dreams are usually quite frightening for the dreamer and may even leave feelings of discomfort during the day. They may be very vivid with physical or tactile sensations of movement, heat, cold, wind, wetness.

The inclination of most dreamers is to find the day residue—some image that is related to those in the dream—and say that was why they had the dream. I say, "Okay. That's layer one. But why these images?" I will explore with the dreamer how this metaphor represents how he is feeling about his life. What feels disastrous? What is the impending catastrophe in your life now that would devastate, flood you, or tear apart your sense of security? If your job is in danger due to downsizing or layoffs, you may feel this would be a personal disaster to your survival. You might also feel the events are out of your control and impossible to prevent, just as you feel about natural disasters. On the other hand, you may have some control over keeping your job or not because your danger of being fired is based on your behavior and skills. In that case, you might be taking action in the dream to minimize your risks against the storms such as seeking shelter or boarding up your house. These actions could represent your ability to take control of the "deadly forces" in your work environment.

Of course, these same images may be used as symbols of other personal tragedies such as divorce, being sued, loss of loved ones.

With disaster dreams, examine your feelings toward this particular kind of disaster. Note that each of these disasters has a different feel to it, and perhaps a personal reaction for the dreamer. Observe what action you take in the dream and how this might be telling you what you can do to improve your situation in your waking life. If you are behaving in a hopeless or helpless manner in the dream, the message could possibly be telling you to be more proactive in your life before you end up in a disaster.

TRY THIS

If your disaster dream left you feeling upset and/or helpless, reenter the dream in active imagination (see chapter 5). Change the ending so that you feel safe, secure, competent—whatever was unsatisfactory in the dream.

EMBARKING ON A JOURNEY, TRIP, OR EXPEDITION

Life is a journey. In dreams, we use this metaphor in some literal way, depicted as a trip or expedition. Our excursion might be a safari, a cruise, or some other voyage. We might be at an airport or be waiting for a sailboat. In each of these is the metaphor of how we travel through life—with ease, trepidation, or having made many preparations. What do you bring with you? Do you feel prepared or unprepared for this journey? Do you dread it? Or do you look forward to it with anticipation? What must you do to get ready?

Remember that the dream is a status report about your present life. There will be information to tell you what you are doing or not doing to achieve your fullest potential and life satisfaction. When scrutinized on the several layers of dreamwork (see step 12 of 20 Steps for Dreamwork in Appendix D), it might tell you what your life mission is.

On occasion, dreams of journeys or waiting for a vehicle such as a ship may be a preparation for death. In elderly people or others whose death is at hand, dreams of waiting for a boat to take them to the other side (or some variation of this) are not unusual. Sometimes they recognize their deceased relatives on the ship. Commonly, they are not afraid but are preparing to greet these family members. Rather than dreaming of literal death (which is usually a metaphor) they dream of taking a trip, which becomes a metaphor of death.

TRY THIS

If your life is a journey, what kind of journey is it? Make up a fairy tale of a journey that represents your life so far. What lies ahead? What do you see? What emotions come up?

VIVID COLORS OR OTHER SENSORY EXPERIENCES

Dreamers frequently want to know what particular colors mean in dreams. Since all symbols are used in a personal way, we must ask the dreamer what these colors mean to him or her. What do these colors make you think of? How is this color an expression of the feelings in the dream? You might want to ask yourself, What is colorful in my life? Do I refer to my life or someone else's as colorful or with many strong feelings?

If you are having tactile sensations or can smell or taste in your dreams, examine the details of these very vivid dreams for forceful metaphors and important information.

TRY THIS

Get into a relaxed state and imagine a scene in which you are the observer. What do you see? What are the first colors you notice? How do these colors reflect your current emotional state?

HOUSE BREAK-INS

Dreaming that someone is breaking into your home can be very frightening. Sometimes the dreamer will know she is in bed and have a clear expectation the intruder will rape or kill her. The sense of danger can be mild to terrifying, even waking the dreamer up in the moment of greatest fear. The dreamer could ask herself the following:

Who or what feels like an intrusion in my life? What is my reaction in the dream and how is that an expression of how I was feeling about events of the previous day? What does the person breaking in want? Is the person who breaks in a stranger or someone I know? This may be a statement about someone in your life who you feel is intruding on you or crossing over your boundaries.

What do I believe is going to happen? Am I worried about money or jewelry or papers? Do I think more about protecting myself or the welfare of others in my household? This dream may be telling you something about your waking concerns or fears for your safety. That safety may be more emotional and psychological than physical.

On the other hand, you might ask, Am I trying to break into something such as a business or entertainment career? How is this dream intruder some part of me? You may be seeing your own dishonesty or how you are pushing the limits of someone else's boundaries. If you look at this as doing it to yourself where you are both the intruder and the person who is fearful, then you might see how you are stretching your own boundaries. This may or may not be positive.

TRY THIS

Imagine you have just had a very scary dream of someone trying to break into your house. Who is it? Male or female? What do you think they want? What's the first thing that comes to mind? What does this say about your values and concerns at this moment? Remember that the dream (or this waking fantasy) is only a snapshot and not a global statement about your character or beliefs.

UNKNOWN, EXOTIC SETTINGS

If your dream takes place in a setting that is completely unfamiliar to you, if it is exotic or strange or curious, ask yourself how this feels. What happened during the day before the dream that had these same feelings? Where was I that seemed strange, curious, or exotic—the way described in the dream environment. In what way might I be feeling like a stranger in a strange land?

These bizarre settings sometimes provide the impetus for innovative fiction writing or science fiction. Such originality can be a stimulus for your creativity.

TRY THIS

On paper, describe your exotic setting in meticulous detail. Then, using colored pens or pastels, draw some dominant feature of this setting. What emotions and memories arise from these images?

TALKING ANIMALS, QUOTES

It is not at all unusual for animals to talk in dreams. These may be your pets in waking life or other animals and creatures from your dreamscape. A dream animal is often a part of the dreamer represented by a particular animal. If the animal is speaking, you might want to ask questions. (See Gallegos, *The Personal Totem Pole*, 1985.)

Remember that these messages come from your unconscious where you are more wise and clear than you are in waking life. Take heed of the message and examine it with your waking common sense and knowledge of the facts.

Similarly, if you hear a message in a dream, this might be a summary of the most important message the dream is bringing you. What does this mean when looked at in the light of your previous day? What might the message be saying in the larger scope of your life's purpose and meaning?

TRY THIS

Imagine yourself as this speaking character in your dream. In the voice of your animal or the speaker whose quote you have, give a speech to yourself. Say what your waking self needs to hear and say it with authority and conviction. What comes out? Does this feel like wisdom or like someone you wouldn't want to listen to? How about both?

ALIENS, SPACE CREATURES, AND UFOS

Our dreams reflect our culture, technology, and waking images, as well as our beliefs and expectations. If you follow the controversies about aliens, read science fiction, or watch movies about these subjects, you are likely to use these images in your dreams. In an era when one's daily images were more likely to be agricultural, dreams would have contained those images. I'm sure people didn't dream about computer terminals and keyboards before they had computers.

If you're dreaming about aliens or extraterrestrials, ask yourself how these figures might be disowned parts of yourself. Are you feeling like an alien in some way? Do you use this word when referring to someone who is not native born to this country? Do you have concerns about immigration? Are you an illegal alien?

If you are being abducted by aliens, how does this feel? Do you feel violated, as if you are being manipulated, coerced, or forced into something you don't want to do? How does this speak to your present life circumstances, your relationships, and your work?

If it's a UFO in the dream, how do you describe it? What is a UFO? What has come into your life that seems otherworldly or foreign? Do you feel as if you are so out of place that you are not from this planet? What in your life feels like a mystery or is unidentified?

As with the earlier discussions of whether a dream might be evidence of a memory surfacing, some people might wonder whether a dream of being abducted by aliens is documentation of an event in reality. Because these experiences and dreams do not offer up tangible evidence from a scientific point of view, we must look at them in another way. Keith Thompson (see pages 121–34, *Spiritual Emergency,* Grof and Grof, editors, 1989) addresses this issue by seeing the UFO encounter as a crisis of transformation. As with dreams of these experiences and other vivid dreams, the individual may be in the process of personal transformation. After this experience, the individual no longer views humanity and his place in it as he did before. The old constraints imposed by indoctrinated beliefs and cultural norms may no longer apply or seem relevant. The person has stepped out of the old boundaries, just as one might after having had a visionary or religious experience.

NUMBERS

When numbers appear in dreams, the dreamer is often propelled into buying lottery tickets. More than one person has reported getting their winning numbers in a dream. But I would also like to know how many people played these numbers and didn't win.

When I work with numbers in dreams, I ask the dreamer what comes to mind when hearing these numbers, just as I do with any other dream element. If it's a series of numbers, I will ask about these as ages in the person's life. What is the significance of this number to the dreamer? Does it represent the size of her family, the year she married or made some other life change? Perhaps the numbers are markers in some way. One woman told a dream of being on an elevator in a hotel. She got off at the third, eighth, and eleventh floors. We played around with these numbers, writing them as dates, ages, etc. The dreamer had an *aha* of recognition when she realized that these were the years in her marriage when she had begun an affair. She had gotten off the straight path of the elevator (marriage). An elevator as a symbol of marriage also captured her sense of being confined and limited. She felt boxed in.

If you have numbers in your dream, it is important to hear how you first report them. The number 230 might be said *two-thirty* or *two hundred and thirty*. The former would make me wonder if this represented a time of day. It might also be a price for something. In dream groups, we play with the possibilities and the associations of the dreamer to see what significance this holds. Is it a time? a year? a date? an age? Perhaps the number is a play on words, such as bringing something to four might really mean bringing it to the fore.

See what you get when you experiment with writing and speaking the numbers that come up in a dream. And of course, play the lottery with them. As in all of life, you can't win if you don't play.

While these dreams are all quite common, not everyone will have them. An individual dreamer might have a variety of common dreams, but not experience others. Another person will have a different constellation of repeating themes and images. The suggestions and questions above are only that: suggestions for working with these common dream themes. Each dreamer must explore what these dreams mean to him or her, and to understand the meaning and implications in current life.

·*ten*·

Dreams and Creativity

BECAUSE DREAMS COME FROM THE SAME source as all our creativity, working regularly with dreams releases this wealth of originality or brings it close enough to the surface to use for creative projects. Many authors report first meeting a fictional character in a dream. Scientists and mathematicians often find solutions to the problems they are researching. Some of the most important scientific breakthroughs have come from dream material.

You can actively engage the help of your dreams to support and stimulate your creative projects. Many of the people in my dream groups are artists and writers, and their dreams have provided them with ideas for future projects. Their dreams suggest ways to get unstuck creatively and help them solve creative dilemmas. One woman felt her artistic vision was activated by the images of her dreams and she put these into her quilts. Another dream spurred a man to work in clay rather than words, and he was astounded by the talent he discovered in his hands.

We can hear imagination and poetic creativity at work in the

dream of a woman in her forties. She was terminally ill with cancer and about to begin a second round of chemotherapy when she
had the following dream:

> I am looking at a beautiful, old home. The city said
> it must be torn down. As I watch, a wrecking ball is hit-
> ting it. I know there are treasures inside: antiques and
> lovely woodwork.

This dream was a poetic image that captured her fears and the
reality of chemotherapy treatment. She had been very sick from its
side effects during her first round of therapy. She feared the treatment didn't distinguish between her cancer and her healthy parts;
it wrecked them all.

At the same time, the dream expressed what she saw as the
treasures inside herself and the sadness she felt about coming to
the end of her life. This dream may have expressed her expectation of her death, which followed two months later.

Another woman used her dream of angels in a garden as the
images for her next painting. One man in a dream group hears
music in his dreams and is often singing a song when he wakes up.
The song has a message in its lyrics, which is why he chose it, but
he also uses these melodies for his musical creativity and composition. The characters in your dreams, in addition to being parts of
you, can also become fictional characters in your novels and short
stories.

From the beginning, I have said I believe dreaming is a doorway. We walk through the dream to discover aspects of ourselves
we didn't know; we gain other views on our relationships, other
people, our behavior. We may even learn our place in the universe
so that we might formulate a mission to accomplish our purpose
here. As we have already seen in the chapters on dreamwork tech-

niques, dreams can be seen as a jumping-off point for other kinds of inner work.

As we have seen, dreams come from the unconscious, the deeper layers of our psyche or soul. Creativity comes from this same source.

Carl Jung called the parts of ourselves that were revealed in dreams elements of our Shadow—with a capital *S*. Most people assume the Shadow is the dark side of the personality where our anger, revenge, envy, and runaway lust reside. But for Jung and other modern psychologists, the Shadow contains all that we deny about ourselves—including those positive parts that we haven't allowed expression.

Roberto Assagioli called these subpersonalities. This may be a childlike part in the positive sense of playful, open, and able to experience awe and wonder.

For many, the Shadow includes our most creative urges to draw, dance, sing, paint, write, sculpt, compose music. Many of us hold these parts down, claiming we have no talent, or no time to pursue these arts. We tell ourselves we can't do it because it isn't practical. We'll never make money at making art. It's frivolous and juvenile.

Silly stuff. So just forget about it. Sound familiar? From my work with dreams and the creativity they contain, I am convinced that keeping down these creative parts of ourselves is dangerous. For some of us, unexpressed creativity can make us physically and mentally ill. I believe that much of the depression, uneasiness, and unhappiness we see in our society is a result of shutting down our creative impulses. This doesn't mean we run from our responsibilities or not work for a living so we can be artists. But to deny time for creativity makes for a lot of unhappy people. The energy it takes to stuff down those desires and other so-called unacceptable feelings drains us and makes us feel tired and withered. I encourage my students and workshop participants to express their creativity and not worry about the quality of the results. It's the process that counts. Writing a poem, drawing with crayons, or sculpting in clay or Play-Doh feels wonderful. I encourage you to try it—especially if you haven't done this since elementary school. Before the days of modern technology and the conveniences of appliances, people made time to do craft work: to carve wood, make patchwork quilts. Unlike most of us, their work and their art were connected. How did they have time when they had to feed and clothe ten children? Certainly, we can find the time, too.

As dreams put what seem to be unrelated pictures and ideas together to tell us something new, creative work is also about new combinations and concepts. Many people believe we need to be in an altered state of consciousness to be creative, but few realize how accessible these states are in our everyday lives.

Dreaming is surely different from our waking consciousness. Most people think of themselves as having only three states of consciousness: awake, asleep, and dreaming. But when we are awake, there are literally thousands of altered states of consciousness (ASCs) that most people experience regularly.

When you're reading a book and you stop hearing the sounds around you, even to the point of not hearing your name called, you are in an altered state. The kind of dazed-out state most people experience while watching television or a movie is another. If you are driving and find yourself at your destination without remembering the trip, you were in an altered state. Extreme agitation, grogginess, blind rage, and completely riveted focus of sensuality and pleasure during lovemaking are all altered states.

Most of us enter and leave these many states without conscious awareness or will. We get caught up in the emotions of a movie, a religious service, or a motivational seminar. We may not even be aware of the manipulative tactics others use to create these states in us for their control or personal gain. This is especially disturbing when these methods are used by charlatans of all varieties to entice, seduce, control, and exploit others (Singer and Lalich, 1995).

Is dreaming the same or different from all these other states? Dreaming is one of many of these states, a natural altered state of consciousness. But even dreaming has various levels, as we've seen. Conscious dreaming, also called lucid dreaming, is different from the dreams we have when we don't know we are dreaming.

While we have seen we can have some control over our dreams by increasing dream recall or improving the likelihood of experiencing a lucid dream, we can also induce altered states or use the content of our dreams to tap into creativity or to nurture our projects in new and creative ways.

In many cultures of the world, people induce altered states for the purpose of having visions to aid an individual in distress or to help the community. These methods include drumming, commonly used by Native American and African cultures as part of their religious and spiritual ceremonies. Some people use chanting, practiced by many throughout the world, but known to Westerners by the Eastern philosophies that brought them here. Dancing, too, can create an altered state of consciousness, giving rise to feelings and images that might not surface through the usual means of talking and thinking.

TRY THIS

(For your first time with this exercise, try it alone if you are inhibited by the idea of doing it in a group.) Choose some rhythmic music you like, preferably without lyrics. Or purchase a drumming tape, recorded for this purpose. Sit comfortably. In time to the music, begin by tapping your hands and feet, moving your body to the music. If you want to add vocal sounds, do so. As you feel yourself being more and more carried into the music, get up and dance or move without thinking about what you're doing.

After dancing, make a journal entry about this experience.

What was it like? Did you feel different from the way you usually do when dancing? Did your body loosen? What feelings or thoughts came up for you? Did your movements express a particular constellation of feelings such as sadness or joy or discovery?

Relaxation opens us to many altered states of consciousness, including helping us to recall our dreams. By bringing ourselves to a relaxed state before embarking on inner work or a creative project, we facilitate the opening of unconsciousness processes. Once relaxed, we are able to go inward and tune in to our thoughts and feelings, which we may be unable to do when we are in the midst of noise, activity, and the company of others. Many of our physical tensions are a defense against our experiencing what we consider to be unacceptable thoughts or emotions. Relaxing our bodies intentionally will help us plumb the depths of our psyche to reach our truest selves. Conversely, if you do dreamwork and other kinds of inner work (journal writing, drawing, meditating), you will find yourself more frequently calm and relaxed as well as more creative, open, and ready to learn.

There are many excellent relaxation tapes available. If you like, you can make your own by using the relaxation suggestions in Appendix Q and reading them into a tape recorder.

Meditation also provides a way to prepare yourself to enter a more creative state as well as to grow spiritually and psychologically. The physiological and psychological benefits of meditation have been well documented.

If you have never meditated and would like to learn more about it, I recommend Lawrence LeShan's excellent beginner's text, *How to Meditate*. This little book is a gem of basic meditation techniques. Jack Kornfield and Ram Dass have also written extensively on the subject of meditation as a spiritual path with its attendant pitfalls. For these and other interesting meditation techniques, see the books, in the bibliography, by Starhawk and Diane Mariechild.

I am often asked about the relationship between dreaming and meditation. Are the images and feelings that rise up in meditation the same as those we have while dreaming? The origin of both of these experiences is thought to be the unconscious. However, while meditating, we still have some control over what we allow to rise to consciousness. If we have a thought we don't like, we can shut it off, or push it out of awareness. We can actively decide to think about something else, or bring ourselves back to our mantra or the visual focus of meditation. By contrast, while dreaming we have the lid off. Often, the dream takes us down paths we would never venture toward when meditating. If we are lucid in the dream, we might be able to turn off the scary part of a dream or wake ourselves up. More frequently, however, the dream takes us where it will. So, in a way, the dream stretches our boundaries and our emotional experience in a way that beginning meditators are not likely to experience. Stretching yourself is exactly what creativity is about; it's how we get to something new, fresh, or original. In the suggestible frame of mind that meditation and relaxation creates, we can overcome our usual blocks to the creative process. Creativity means dropping some of our usual inhibitions, and our dreams will help us do this.

GUIDED IMAGERY

At workshops and seminars, retreats and schools, guided imagery has become a popular method for doing inner work and stimulating creativity. Seen as an extension of dreamwork, these techniques may supplement the exploration of dreams and draw out stories, images, and artistic expressions of all kinds. When working with guided imagery, it is important to use a script that does not contain suggestions for a certain outcome. The ambiguity of the script and outcome releases your own creative and unconscious possibilities.

To do guided imagery alone, you may write or choose a script that appeals to you and then record it so you can play it for yourself for creative exploration. See *Mind Games* by Robert Masters and Jean Houston for additional scripts.

If you have ever wished you were more creative or have wanted to improve your creativity in a particular area (sculpting, painting, drawing, dance, composing music, writing), use the dream incubation technique to tell yourself you will have a dream to stimulate your creativity. At bedtime, set out your artistic (or writing) supplies and space to be ready when you wake up. As you go to sleep, imagine yourself immersed in your creative project, doing exactly what you would be doing if you had been involved in this art form for twenty years. See your hands move with precision and confidence or see the words flow out of your fingertips and onto the page or keyboard. Expect a dream to nourish this creative flow. Whatever you dream, see it as endorsing your request. When you get up in the morning, engage in the imagined artistic activity no matter what you dreamed.

DREAMS AS INSPIRATION

When you give yourself the gift of a particularly vivid dream or a dream that makes a big impression on you because of its emotional content, this is an excellent opportunity to use this dream for a creative leap. Because these vivid and sometimes disturbing dreams are an important message from your unconscious to your conscious mind, they carry with them the energy and force that provoke most creative projects. Did you ever wonder how someone finds the energy and perseverance to write a book or an epic poem? Or to work on a single painting or a sculpture for months? What fuels the project is often a burning need to express something. What is being expressed through the art form is sometimes not even clear to the artist at the time of the work. The artistic process is the unfolding and bringing the material to consciousness and to resolution. It is for these reasons that the dreams that grab your attention can be used as an excellent source of inspiration or as a stimulus for that creative leap. The process of deciphering the dream's scattered and seemingly weakly linked images makes meaning of them.

TRANSFORMING DREAMS INTO ART
TRY THIS

Choose a dream that was particularly vivid. This may be a recent or old dream. Whether or not you feel you understand the dream, make a list of its elements, as suggested in chapter 3:

place or setting
strongest emotions
theme or major idea
actions
images
character(s)—animals or people
sounds, rhythm
sensations, or texture or touch
dialogue, conversation
messages
phrases or single words
dream title
movement or physical orientation
smells
tastes

From all these elements, use one as a jumping-off point for a creative work. Start small. If you have an image of an apple in a dream, try writing a poem or a paragraph with an apple as the central metaphor. Where does the image of "apple" take you in your personal history and what stories does it make you want to tell? For one person, it might lead to an outdoor scene of apple orchards and picking apples. For another, to baking apple pies, starting with the textures and smells of peeling apples. Perhaps you thought of an apple for the teacher. Is your apple red or green? Why one or the other?

You might consider drawing this apple or painting it. How about molding the apple out of the new plastics that come in a large assortment of colors? These are available in any art-supply store. Note that though you may have started with an image of an apple, you might then want to explore texture, shape, size, smell, or even the sound you hear when you bite into an apple. As with any creative project, engage all your senses. Did you think of how apples hanging on a tree might move in the wind? Does this suggest movement in dance?

Any of these avenues can be used as clues to other as-yet-uncovered layers of the dream, but they are also opportunities to tap into your own inner oil wells of talent and wisdom.

TRY THIS

Begin a habit of looking for images that appear in your dreams in newspapers, magazines, catalogues, or advertisements in the mail. Most people have certain symbols that show up again and again in their dreams. They are then surprised when these same symbols seem to be frequently seen in their daily life. Clip these pictures and start a collection of photos, drawings, words that catch your eye. Then assemble them in a collage, possibly adding other objects that you feel belong such as small stones, leaves, feathers, sand or gravel, personal photos. Let these come together without a lot of conscious deliberation. Trust your unconscious and let your creativity lead you where it will.

*Note: This collage of dream symbols will also help you remember your dream signs and improve your ability to dream lucidly (see chapter 5).

USING DREAMS TO SUPPORT CREATIVE PROJECTS
TRY THIS

Your dream characters are an excellent beginning for a creative work. Certainly, your dream has already begun the creative process by suggesting a character to you or using a person (or more likely a composite person) from your waking life. What is in the heart of this person? If he or she is acting menacingly in the dream, what is the message of that behavior? All behavior is communication—in dreams and in waking life. Let this character speak to you as the author and tell you how she or he wants to be understood and portrayed. Is this dream figure angry with you because it feels misunderstood? What might you do to understand it better?

This is another way of doing a dialogue with a dream character (see chapter 5). This time, more than understanding the meaning of the dream, you are now able to use the character in a creative work such as a short story or novel.

You might even ask this character to give you advice about your plot, ideas, or another character in the fictional piece you want to write.

TRY THIS

Choose a particularly scary character or animal in a dream. Write in the first person as this figure and allow its dark and fearsome nature to show itself fully. Be as gory and violent as the creature calls for. This is another way to ventilate your own dark side while safely containing it.

In Stephen King's *Danse Macabre*, in the chapter on horror

fiction, he addresses this issue when he states, ". . . the primary duty of literature [is] to tell us the truth about ourselves by telling us lies about people who never existed." In dreams, too, we see those aspects of ourselves crying out for expression. By making art of these elements, we give them the honor due them.

Roger Walsh, in *The Spirit of Shamanism*, says, "Shamans may be especially able to create meaningful patterns from unclear data—that is, they tend to organize ambiguous experiences into coherent meaningful images." This ability may be compared to the art of dreamwork where we can see the possibilities for practical meaning that dreams offer. The shaman asks for visions and messages that call upon the Higher Self or other channels of wisdom. As Westerners become more interested in Native cultures, many more people are exploring the experiences of shamanic journeying using techniques similar to those used in dreamwork, seeing each of the elements metaphorically as well as literally.

All of us can use the images of our dreams to take us on adventures inside ourselves and into the world of art where we might not otherwise travel.

METAPHOR AS ART; ART AS METAPHOR

Many times throughout this book, we have seen how our dreams have a literary and poetic quality. The dream is a metaphor telling us about our life, just as art has a metaphorical quality to tell us about life and our struggles being human.

·eleven·

Conclusion

ACTING ON THE DREAM MESSAGE

Throughout this book, the perspective on dreaming has been to find the useful, practical applications for dream messages. While the exploration of dreams can be fun, exciting, and moving, I believe dreamwork should have a purpose or goal.

Many of us do inner work of various kinds for years and years. We stay in therapy for decades, go on retreats and quests to find enlightenment. In the search for peace and fulfillment outside or out there somewhere, we may lose the way to our true self that we dream every night. After all this work and effort, we are sometimes able to list our shortcomings and know the origins of our quirks and phobias, but not much has changed.

What is the value of a psychological insight if we continue in the same patterns of thinking and behavior? What benefit do we get if we remain as stuck as ever in our stuff? What value is there if the exploration adds to our feeling helpless, hopeless, and a victim?

For me, the purpose of dreamwork is to use the messages for personal growth. I like psychologist Michael F. Hoyt's characterization of himself as "expander" rather than "shrink." In his collection of papers, "Brief Therapy and Managed Care" (1995), he emphasizes how psychological work can help you grow and expand. To his patients, he says, "The way I can do that is to help you recognize and understand the barriers you may be creating psychologically that interfere with your being who you want to be." Dreamwork is one path to finding out how we can fully be who we are when we are most authentic and comfortable with ourselves with more choices open to us. Dreamwork can awaken us to live more lucidly and sensually with the joyful pleasure and acceptance of who we really are.

At the end of each dream's analysis, here are some questions I recommend you ask yourself.

Why did I have this dream now?

What important message is this dream giving me?

What does the dream tell me about myself?

What unfinished business is the dream highlighting?

What can I do to act on the message of the dream?

What action might make this issue more complete or give it closure?

Does the dream offer a hint of what this action might be?

Sometimes, when I talk about acting on the dream's message, people become anxious. If I have a sexual dream where I engage in behaviors I find abhorrent in waking life, does that mean I need to do them? If I have a violent dream, should I act this out?

Of course not. The action is based on the metaphor, not the literal images of the dream. In the opening chapter, a dream I had about how I was being harshly critical with a friend told me clearly to be aware of my behavior, to stop this pattern, and to apologize and recognize my friend's hurt feelings.

If you feel your dream is telling you to take a dramatic action such as divorce or quitting a job, I recommend incubating more dreams on the subject you think the dream is about. Certainly, always use your waking powers of discrimination and critical analysis to see and make your choice of action. You might hear this process of dreamwork plus critical thinking as the mix of intuition and reason, both of which are necessary to live fully.

Many people are puzzled by what action to take after a dream. A dreamer may have recurrent dreams about a deceased loved one. What action is the dream pointing toward? The emotions and the ending of the dream might be clues. Frequently, the message for the dreamer is that the grief work around the loss of this person is incomplete. Maybe there are unshed tears. In the dream, you might go to this lost person to say something that was never said in waking life. You might want to hear something from the deceased—perhaps, "I love you," or "I admire you." What might you want to hear? What is unfinished? Here, again, we can examine how a letter or a ritual might be the suitable action to bring closure (see chapter 5).

Often, the only action to take might be to change your attitude or perspective. What are you telling yourself that you can change? If I see something as a catastrophe, maybe the dream hints that this is an opportunity or a blessing in disguise. How does this crisis or nightmare offer something to learn?

Stephen Covey reminds us that sometimes we can't choose what happens to us, but we can always choose our attitude toward it. Aldous Huxley said, "Experience is not what happens to a man [*sic*]. It is what a man does with what happens to him."

We have the power to give meaning and emphasis to the events of our lives. We can let our traumas define us or we can use them to be better, to grow, and to have more understanding of ourselves and others. Our dreams will point out our defects in character, the ways we cheat ourselves and others so that we can make a conscious decision to change. We will be more aware of our shortcomings as well as our strengths. We can amplify what works and eliminate what doesn't.

You can use your dreams to validate a poor self-image or you can use them as stepping-stones to move toward being all you can be—dreaming your real self. The choice is yours.

As we depart for our individual dream journeys, I wish you courage and persistence and a boundless sense of humor. May you translate the wisdom of your dream messages into a way to be more truly all you were meant to be, whatever that means to you.

KEY TO APPENDICES

A. Benefits of Working with Dreams
B. 10 Reasons Why We Don't Remember Our Dreams
C. 10 Steps to Improve Dream Recall
D. 20 Steps for Dreamwork
E. Dream Work Sheet
F. Suggestions for Using the Dream Work Sheet
G. 10 Basic Tips for Dreamwork
H. Myths About Dreams
I. Dream Incubation
J. Common Dreams and Key Questions
K. Steps for Lucid Dreaming
L. Steps for Conquering Nightmares and Recurrent Dreams
M. Steps for Getting Back into the Dream
N. Norms (General Directions) for Dream Groups
O. Gestalt Empty Chair Technique
P. Suggestions for Dealing with Insomnia
Q. Relaxation Exercise
R. Meditation Instruction

S. Meditation of the White Light
T. Dream Test

APPENDIX A
Benefits of Working with Dreams

- Taps into our creativity and originality.
- Gives us a current picture of our lives.
- Brings us closer to our unconscious processes.
- Makes us aware of our strengths and resources.
- Points out our defects of character and our shortcomings.
- Brings us to a closer awareness of our deepest feelings.
- Sheds light on the character of others whom we have dismissed, ignored, or denied.
- Clarifies the present state of our relationships.
- Assists us in problem solving and decision making.
- Encourages us to overcome our fears.
- Cautions us about our risks and dangers.
- Tells us about the health of our bodies.
- Helps us integrate traumas, losses, failures, successes.
- Points the way to being our truest, most authentic selves.
- Centers and stabilizes us emotionally.
- Sharing dreams with others provides a path to intimacy and knowledge of one another.
- Taps into our higher selves, our source of wisdom.

APPENDIX B
Ten Reasons Why We Don't Remember Our Dreams

1. Dreams come to us in a jumbled, nonlinear form, which is not the way we are used to thinking. These confusing im-

ages make it difficult to relate the dream (even to ourselves) in a chronological and coherent fashion.

2. Our culture doesn't honor the dream as valuable information or take it seriously. Most people assume dreams are meaningless and see exploring them as superstitious or worse.

3. People don't pay much attention to us when we want to tell our dreams. They shrug them off and don't ask us to elaborate on the details, nor do they question what meanings the dream might hold.

4. We are often embarrassed or repulsed by the content of our dreams so we often don't really want to remember them. Wanting to remember is frequently a prerequisite to remembering. Attending to our dreams immediately increases recall.

5. We are afraid others will think we are crazy or weird because of the dreams we have.

6. Our nightmares frighten us and make us wonder if we are mentally disturbed or potentially dangerous.

7. Most dreams are not emotionally charged or terrifying so we are more likely to sleep through them without waking up. Rather, we remember the ones that are unpleasant and frightening and then dismiss them from our minds because they are so unpleasant.

8. On awakening, we begin our daily responsibilities immediately rather than waking up slowly with time to think out what was on our minds. Dreams and nightmares are elusive and disappear on awakening if we don't make an effort to remember them.

9. Some myths about dreams discourage us from exploring them.

10. Our lives are so busy, few of us take time for contemplation of our dreams or private thoughts.

APPENDIX C
Ten Steps to Improve Dream Recall

1. Keep a notebook and pen at your bedside every night and during naps if you take them. This is especially true on your days off from work, when on vacation, or when away from home for any reason. People often have more dream recall when in a new or different sleep environment.
2. Go to sleep with the conscious intention of remembering your dreams. Say aloud before going to sleep: "I will dream tonight and I will remember my dreams in the morning. I'll write down my dream as soon as I wake up." Imagine yourself writing down your dreams.
3. Avoid using alarms or clock radios to wake. Try to stay in the same physical position in bed without jumping up.
4. Avoid the use of alcohol and tranquilizers, both of which inhibit dreaming and dream recall. This is equally true of illegal and hallucinogenic drugs. Some medications such as antipsychotics will also reduce dreaming, but others can cause nightmares. Consult your physician before discontinuing or reducing the dosage of any prescription drugs.
5. Stay in bed a few minutes upon awakening and ask yourself what you were just thinking about. Where was I? What was just happening?
6. Write down whatever comes to mind even if it seems completely senseless and bizarre. A short note is better than nothing at all. A fragment of a dream when recorded and reviewed will often bring back an entire dream. Dream fragments by themselves can be rich with information.
7. While still in bed, go over the dream several times in your mind to memorize the events of the dream, no matter how bizarre or disturbing. The more disturbing or odd a dream is, the more important the message to yourself is.
8. At your first opportunity, record the dream in its entirety on

paper or by tape recorder. Just record the dream without thoughts about its interpretation or analysis. Give as many details as possible.

9. Drink a large amount of water before bedtime. When you wake up to urinate, try to capture what you were dreaming and make some notes. A few key words or phrases are often enough to help you recall your dream in the morning.

10. Be patient and keep trying. The more you want to remember your dreams and the more you pay attention to the ones you have, the more dreams you'll remember. When you have too many to record and work on, commit to working on at least one dream per week in detail.

APPENDIX D
Twenty Steps for Dreamwork

1. Record the dream in specific detail as soon as possible.
2. What are the main events of the dream?
3. What are your dominant feelings during the dream? at the end of the dream?
4. Describe each person, animal, place, or thing.
5. What do these descriptions remind you of?
6. What are your feelings related to each description?
7. What were you thinking about when you went to bed before the dream?
8. What were the main events of your day?
9. What happened the day of the dream that left you with feelings similar or in contrast to those of your dream?
10. What do your descriptions from the dream sound like in your current life?
11. Summarize the dream in one sentence.
12. How is this a *metaphor* for your

♦ relationships? (friendships, children, lover, spouse, co-workers)
♦ family of origin and childhood wounds?
♦ inner self? mental/emotional state?
♦ professional/work life?
♦ spiritual life?
♦ personal history and family of origin?
♦ body's health?

13. What subpersonalities or aspects of your Shadow does the dream expose?
14. What new information does this dream bring to light?
15. How is this a more honest statement about your current situation?
16. What action does the dream call for?
17. What other possible meanings does this dream hold?
18. If this were someone else's dream, how would you interpret it? What questions might you want to ask this dreamer?
19. How do you feel now?
20. Phrase a specific question to ask for another dream.
    Further work:
    ♦ dialogue with dream characters and animals
    ♦ draw, paint, or sculpt the dream images and/or feelings
    ♦ dramatize and exaggerate the dream actions and feelings
    ♦ use dream stories and images for creative inspiration

APPENDIX E
Dream Work Sheet

Date and time of dream: Title:

Events of the dream:

Feelings in the dream:

List of elements:

Associations:

Events of the previous day:

Possible interpretations:

Action to take?

Incubation for future dream:

APPENDIX F
Suggestions for Using the Dream Work Sheet

If recording dreams by hand, the work sheet can be used with spaces large enough to handwrite in what you want to say. But it is preferable to write in the headings when you are ready to write in each space.

Working at a computer has several advantages over recording dreams in longhand. You can fill in the blanks with as much or as little text as you need. You can also set up the fields in a database and then be able to search your dreams for specific symbols, characters, or other elements that repeat. Seeing this pattern can be helpful in exploring your own growth or how your feelings about something change over time. You can use the report functions with the database to print out only certain fields, such as getting a list of your dream titles and dates.

Whatever style of recording you use, develop it and change it so that it works for you. There is only one correct way to keep a journal or record your dreams: *Your Way!*

APPENDIX G
Ten Basic Tips for Dreamwork

1. Dreams have layers of meanings about all the important areas in your life.
2. When a literal meaning of a dream is valid for the dreamer, that is only the first layer. Look beyond to a metaphorical meaning. For example, if you dream about losing your teeth on a day when you have a dentist's appointment, you might ask how this is about something you can't sink your teeth into, can't swallow, or how you've bit off more than you can chew. If the dreamer says the meaning is obvious, that is only the first layer of meaning.
3. Symbols are always used in a personal and private way, reflecting the individual's experience with the symbols as well as the dreamer's use of language and figures of speech. If you call someone a snake or an animal, that person might show up as one in your dream. As above, look for puns and plays on words in the choice of symbols.
4. Dream characters may represent real people in your life now or in your past, parts of you (subpersonalities or your Shadow), or all of these. Examine each possibility as having not only a separate but also interlocking layers of meaning.
5. Recall of dreams is the conscious awareness of unconscious processes (thoughts, feelings, perceptions). These offer some new information or a new view of your life, your work, or your life purpose, your self-image. Often, this view is a compensation or a balancing assessment of the one you hold in your waking consciousness.
6. All dreams are gifts, especially those that are the most weird, upsetting, or repulsive since they bring us information that needs to be brought into our awareness. When put to use, the wisdom of the dream can save us further pain and anxiety.

7. A dream is a snapshot of the present state of the dreamer's thoughts and feelings at the time of the dream. Never make a dramatic decision (divorce or quit a job) based on the interpretation of a single dream.

8. Record, title, and review your dreams. A review of old dreams will reveal patterns and themes and the way you express meaning through metaphor. Old dreams are often easier to understand because those issues have already been resolved or made conscious.

9. Recurrent dreams have special significance for the dreamer and might be a way the dreamer repeatedly depicts life issues that come up under times of stress, the fear of death, or when the dreamer is feeling vulnerable, exhausted, or insecure.

10. The dreamer is the only one who can decide the correct meaning(s) of the dream. The dreamer's recognition will most often have a physiological component such as blushing, laughing, or gasping when the dreamer makes the connection with waking experiences.

APPENDIX H
Myths About Dreams

Dreams are wishes.
Sometimes. Some dreams reflect wishes or desires, but not all of them do. If you are repulsed or upset by your behavior in a dream or by what someone does to you (rape or attack), don't assume you are wishing this to happen. Perhaps you are expressing your fear of this event, or your unconscious is warning you to be more careful. Or you are the attacker and the dream is allowing you to let off steam in a safe way.

Dreams are about sex and aggression.

Sometimes. The sexual and aggressive images might be metaphors for other areas of life. Dreams are also about the desire to love and be loved, to be generous, to make the world a better place, to be a more spiritual being. Dreams can be about anything we care about.

Dreams take only a second in real time.
Not so. Dreams vary in length. Studies show that dreamers take about as much time in a dream to do something as they would in waking life. Long dreams are as long as they seem.

Dreams are repressed or past-life memories.
Not usually. Occasionally a dream will reflect an old memory, but the content of the dream should NOT be considered an accurate report of past events. Dreams are usually fantastic, and our memories are distorted by the dream process even more than they are by our waking changes to memories. Any uncertain memory can only be verified by the memories and experiences of others who were present at the time or other evidence. Sometimes dreams will bring up old events when we are ready to deal with them because our maturity and understanding help us accept old hurts.

A dream dictionary will tell you what your dream means.
Probably not. Because we all use dream symbols in such a personal and individual way, dream dictionaries are inadequate when we want to understand our dreams. Only the dreamer can say for sure what the dream means or what the emotional and historical relevance of a dream symbol is.

If you die in your dream, you will never wake up.
Not so. Many people have dreams of their own death, see themselves dead, in coffins, their bodies decomposing. These dreams usually refer to metaphorical death, a transformation or change in the person's life. And whoever died in his dream and then told someone what happened?

Dreams are warnings.
Sometimes. Only the dreamer's waking examination of the events in the dream compared to present risks can decide if the dream is a warning. However, if the dreamer feels the dream is a warning, then some protective action is a good idea since our beliefs may influence an outcome.

You can be diagnosed as being mentally ill from your dream.
Not so. The dreams of psychotics are indistinguishable from the dreams of so-called normal persons. Most dreams are weird, bizarre, disjointed, and seemingly nonsensical because of the language of dreams.

Dreamwork can be dangerous without an expert to help.
Not so. Anyone can begin to do dreamwork on her own or work with other interested people who are respectful and curious. As long as you aren't using dreams to "nail" people or yourself, dreamwork can be nurturing, supportive, and an opportunity to improve your relationships and your psychological and spiritual health.

Dreamwork can activate evil forces; there is dangerous power behind dream meanings.
Absolutely not. Dreamwork clearly brings out the best in people and gets them in touch with their Higher Selves. From this wisdom, we can think more clearly, be more honest, generous, and forgiving of ourselves and others. Dreams tell us we have the ability to solve our own problems.

You shouldn't write your dreams down.
Not so. It's best to write dreams down if you want to remember them. Having a record of your dreams will give you something to go back to when you want to see how you're changing and making progress.

The spirits of dead people come to you in dreams.
Maybe—if you believe in spirits or any existence after death.

There is no way to verify this belief, but if you hold it, use this information to your best advantage. Since all dreams are helpful in some way, you can ask and get the benefit of whatever wisdom these spirits have. These figures may also be the way you project your Higher Self or some other aspect of your personality onto others. These deceased persons may also be symbols for other people who are currently in your life.

People who dream a lot have psychological problems.
Not at all. Some of the most creative and inventive minds in history dreamed often and used their dreams to solve problems and come up with solutions to scientific, artistic, and political dilemmas. If you remember many of your dreams, consider yourself fortunate to be close to this wellspring of wisdom and creativity.

Some dreams have no significance at all.
Not so. All dreams, when properly examined, seem to have meaning for the dreamer. If you have many, many dreams, you may want to narrow the scope of your examination to only a few of the most vivid or puzzling dreams if you expect to get anything else done.

Dreams foretell the future or show us events at a distance.
Rarely. Some people state this is often true for their dreams, but I suggest they look at what the dream is telling them about what is happening in their lives at the time of the dream. Most dreams are simply revealing information we have at a deeper or unconscious level. We know what the outcome will be if we continue on a certain course of action and dreams often remind us of this, perhaps as a warning to take better care of our health, our relationships, or our careers. We have more knowledge than we are consciously aware of, and this makes dreams seem more prophetic than they usually are.

People who dream in color are psychologically aware.
Not necessarily. Whether or not you dream in color seems to be a

function of how much you express feelings in your waking life. But people who do dreamwork regularly will report color more and more often—either because they dream more in color as they become more in touch with their feelings, or because doing dreamwork makes us more aware in general.

Nightmares come from eating spicy foods before bedtime.
Yes and no. Any chemical change in the body due to food, drugs, alcohol, medication, or emotional upset will influence our dreaming minds. Whatever you dream, you will gain more by looking at the content and understanding the meaning than writing off the nightmare to an outside cause. The dream still holds meaning for the dreamer regardless of its source.

People who don't dream are either more mentally healthy or more psychologically repressed.
Not necessarily. Everyone dreams. People who don't remember their dreams usually haven't taken the time to remember. Remembering dreams doesn't reflect health or the lack of it. But when you DO remember a dream, you are ready to deal with whatever the dream presents.

You can't program your dreams.
Not so! You *can* program or incubate a dream. You can ask questions, request guidance or advice, solve problems, and make decisions. Techniques for programming your dreams are simple, and they work. Many of the great minds in history have used these methods to get trustworthy information.

When you dream, you are having an out-of-body experience or your soul is traveling.
Maybe. I don't know how anyone could know this. It's more important to ask, "Where am I going and what do I need to know or learn?"

Symbols in dreams are disguises for something the dreamer doesn't want to know or face.
Not so. The symbols you use are the best possible representations to capture the ideas and emotions you hold about the important issues in your life. We use symbols over and over again, even after we know what they mean, so the disguise theory doesn't hold up.

Violent dreams indicate the dreamer's tendency toward violence.
Not necessarily. Only the dreamer can answer whether this is an expression of anger or a fear of someone else's or some other explanation. Sometimes the dream is a ventilation of repressed anger and violence, making acting on these feelings LESS likely. Violence is often a metaphor for how the dreamer feels threatened or violated in some emotional or psychological way.

Dreams are just meaningless snatches of the day's events.
Not so. We use the images and events of our life for our dream story, but that is only the first layer of meaning of a dream. You choose these specific images and symbols because they have meaning to you. You use them in a dream to clarify or elucidate something you need to know NOW, at the time of the dream.

Nightmares indicate deep psychological problems.
Not so. Many people have nightmares that might simply be dreams with the volume turned up. They often indicate a problem that needs to be addressed, but they do not predict or indicate pathology by themselves. Some people with deep psychological problems don't remember their dreams at all and some healthy, well-functioning people have frequent nightmares.

Dreams have only one true meaning.
Absolutely not. A single dream is layered with meanings. Each dream is a metaphor for all the important issues in your life: your self-image, work, loves and friendships, your spiritual goals, your physical health and psychological state. Every dream can be ex-

amined on each of these levels. Only the dreamer knows what meanings make sense.

Only a dream expert can say what a dream means.
Not so. Only the dreamer knows what the dream means. Anything anyone else says about your dream, including the "experts," can only be a projection of their own issues onto your dream.

APPENDIX I
Dream Incubation

It is possible to request a dream on a particular subject or a particular person. Perhaps you'd like a solution to a problem that has been plaguing you or you are undecided about courses of action. A relationship may feel problematic and in need of a new viewpoint or strategy for making peace. In any of these cases, you can ask your dreaming self to give you some insight through a dream. The dream might offer new information, clarity, or another way of seeing something old and familiar.

1. Focus on the place where this dream should be to bring you the answer you seek. Engage your five senses to bring your subject most clearly to mind:
   a) the lighting of the place; b) any smells, colors;
   c) any specific image that most puts you in the place.
2. If a person, think about this person as vividly as you can:
   a) recall the sound and pitch of his/her voice;
   b) call up an image of the person in your mind, or gaze at a photo if you have one.
3. If you are trying to solve a problem, write out the problem as you see it with a list of important facts that might impact on the solution.
4. Capture the feeling you have about the subject. For example: fear, confusion, or hope. Let this feeling be a part of

you without trying to change it or stifle it because it gives you discomfort or guilt. Acknowledge the feeling as real without judgment. See the feeling as only a stepping-stone to another emotional or psychological space.

5. Formulate a question or request in the simplest language you can, remembering that the unconscious mind is literal as well as metaphorical. Be as specific as possible. For example: a) I want to see my relationship with Carla more clearly (asking for objective information);

b) show me a new way to understand Carla (other-directed);

c) who am I when I'm with Carla? (inner-directed).

Recite the chosen phrase to yourself throughout the day.

6. Record whatever you remember in the morning, even if your dream appears nonsensical, seems removed from the question or request, or if it seems to be about another subject altogether.

7. No matter what you dream, review it in terms of your request. Most likely, it will be an answer in metaphor or symbol to the question you asked. Though I might dream about my mother or grandmother, the dream is probably telling me something NEW AND HELPFUL about Carla, if that's what I've asked for.

8. *Remember,* you can use this information only to change yourself, not others.

APPENDIX J
Common Dreams and Key Questions

General considerations: Dreams are always about the concerns of our waking minds. Ask yourself how your feelings in the dream are related to your waking life. Dream meanings are revealed through listening to the feelings in the dream. The metaphors the dream uses express these feelings and concerns. Each dream will have several different important meanings.

Houses/buildings: How is the building a representation of your body or your mind? How does the image reflect the state you are in? Is it crumbling, being torn down? Under construction? Have you found treasures or something terrible in the building? What parts of yourself have been hidden from you that this building reveals? A secret? A fear? Do these images feel positive or negative and how are these reflections of how you evaluate yourself at this time? Finding new rooms may be a discovery of new talents and strengths. Or are there creepy inhabitants you don't want to look at?

Forgetting your lines: Do you feel you have flubbed your role in life? What have you forgotten to say that needs to be said? What words are you holding in? In what way do you feel unprepared for a performance? Are you playing a part rather than being yourself?

Unprepared for test, final exam: What do you feel you are being tested for? How important is this? In what way are you feeling unprepared for your present circumstances? How are you feeling scrutinized or examined? In what ways are you afraid of failing?

Can't find your classroom: What are you searching for that you can't find? How important does it feel in the dream? What feels like that in your waking life? What makes you feel lost or out of place? What are you trying to learn?

Bathrooms, toilets: What do you need to unload or spill in your life? Do you have a place where you can let the more repulsive or unattractive parts of yourself be seen? When you unload this *stuff,* do you feel safe or unsafe? Embarrassed or relieved?

Flying: In what way do you feel as if you're flying? Have you had a recent success or accomplishment that once seemed impossible and now feels like an unexpected miracle? How are you feeling good about yourself—so good you'd say you're flying? Is there fear while flying?

Finding money: What have you found recently that feels of value? What unexpected treasure did you find, perhaps in yourself? What did you discover in your life that feels as good as finding money? What nonmonetary riches have come your way?

Getting lost: In what way do you feel lost? What do you mean when you say someone is lost? A lost soul? A lost case? Have you lost an argument or lost hope? Who might be a loser? Would you like to get lost—to have some solitude and quiet?

Losing your car: What would this mean to you? How would your life be if you were without a car? When in the past did you have to do without a car? Are you sloppy about your car security? Are you taking risks with something of value or with your freedom?

Car accidents/cars out of control: How are you not in control of your own movements in life? What course of action are you taking that feels out of control? Are you in the driver's seat in the dream or in your own life? Who is driving the car? If someone else is driving your car, how have you given up your power to this person? Is this a warning to take back your power or a desire to give it up?

Vivid colors, smells, or other sensory experiences: What is colorful in your life? Do you refer to your life or someone else's as colorful or with many strong feelings? What do these colors make you think of? Examine the details of very vivid dreams for forceful metaphors.

Vehicle crashes: What in your life is crashing or feels as if it is about to crash? Are you living in a reckless manner (in activities, finances, romance)? In what way are you headed for a crash? What do you refer to as a *crash*? (taking a crash course, crashing a party, needing to crash/sleep).

Swimming, drowning: What are you drowning in? Do you use this expression to say you are drowning in bills, troubles, people, chores, papers, children? In what way must you *sink or swim*? Are you swimming against the tide (of public opinion) or going with the flow?

Being chased: Who or what in your life is chasing you? What is in your life that haunts or pursues you? Bill collectors? Worries? Someone whom you'd rather avoid? Is the word *chaste*? If you are the pursuer, what are you chasing after in the dream and in life? Do you get it or feel frustrated?

Feeling paralyzed: How are you paralyzed? What can't you bring yourself to do or to act on? What is holding you back? Who or what do you blame for your being immobilized? What are you procrastinating about or afraid of doing? How are you stuck?

Death and dying: (not usually literal death) What is coming to a close or an end in your life? What is dying or needs to die for you to move to the next stage of life? Relationships, friendships may die or feelings and passions may die. What major change are you going through that feels like a dramatic change or a transformation? What's killing you? Are you dead on your feet?

Naked in public: In what way do you feel exposed to others? What does the world now see about you? Does this feel positive or not? Who has exposed you? What aspects of yourself have you revealed to others? Does this feel pleasant, unpleasant, or neutral? Are others naked? In what way are you feeling vulnerable to others?

Falling: In what way have you fallen? Are you falling down on your job? Have you fallen from grace? Fallen off the wagon? Is there an expression where you use the word *fall*? Have you fallen in love? Do your words fall on deaf ears? Do you have a literal concern about a physical fall?

Tornadoes, tidal waves, fires, hurricanes, and other disasters:
What in your life feels like a disaster or an impending disaster?
Does this feel like a powerful, outside source beyond your control?
Are you blown over by something? What burns you? Do you feel
consumed or overwhelmed by something? Does the name of the
dream hurricane have special significance for you?

Unknown, exotic settings: What does this feel like? Are you entering a new and exciting phase of life? Are you about to do something adventurous and different? Are you feeling the need for a
change or fearful of making one? What does your description of
the dream setting reveal to you?

House break-ins: Who or what feels like an intrusion in your life?
What is your reaction in the dream and how is that an expression
of how you were feeling about events of the previous day? What
does the person breaking in want? What do you believe is going
to happen? How is this related to your waking concerns or fears
for your safety? Are you trying to break into something such as a
business or entertainment career?

Erotic and Sexual Dreams: Are you aroused in the dream? Is the
person known to you or a stranger? What would you like the outcome of the dream to be? Are you doing something in the dream
you wouldn't ordinarily do but would like to? Might you be practicing a desire or playing out a fantasy in your dream? Is your partner a likely or unlikely partner? How is the partner a part of you?
Is this a metaphor in sexual language so that it expresses some
feeling other than sex, such as, *Screw you!* Perhaps you are *embracing* an idea or person or taking someone in.

Teeth crumbling or falling out: What is happening to your teeth
and how do you feel about it? Is this about losing face or some
other loss of your self-image? Do you fear a loss of attractiveness?
Do you use expressions with references to teeth such as what you
can't bite into or having *bitten off more than you can chew*? Do you

talk about sinking your teeth into something? Are you or is someone else lying through his teeth? What are your literal, personal concerns about your teeth and their health?

Dead relatives/friends: What is this person like and who in your present situation treats you in the same way or reminds you of this person? How is your present reminding you of your life in the time of your relationship with the deceased person? Do you have unfinished business with this person?

APPENDIX K
Steps for Lucid Dreaming

1. Do reality checks. Is this a dream? Am I dreaming now?
2. Look for inconsistencies or bizarre details in your surroundings.
3. Does this feel familiar? Have I ever dreamed this before?
4. Could these events really happen?
5. These people are dead; I must be dreaming!
6. Transportation? If you're flying without a plane, you're dreaming.
7. Read something (a street sign, a movie marquis, or a book title). If the content changes on a second reading, you're dreaming.
8. Tell yourself you will recognize you are dreaming in the midst of your next dream. Remind yourself of this throughout the day; repeat it as you go to sleep.
9. Know that when you are lucid you will be able to alter the content of your dreams.
10. Once lucid, ask the characters who they are and what they want.

APPENDIX L
Steps for Conquering Nightmares and Recurrent Dreams

1. When does this nightmare or recurrent dream come?
2. Any new chemicals or medications? *ALWAYS consult your doctor before making any changes in your prescription medication.*
3. How is this nightmare a *metaphor* of your present life situation?
4. What most concerns you? How is the dream a statement of this concern?
5. What is the dream telling you that you need to know *now*?
6. What do you need to do or change in your life RIGHT NOW?
7. The dream will stop when you make this important change.

APPENDIX M
Steps for Getting Back into the Dream

1. Return to the sleep position you were in when you woke up. If you can't remember, return to your favorite and most frequent sleep position.
2. Try to recapture the feelings and sensations you were having in the dream when you woke up.
3. Whatever you remember of the dream, replay the events and setting in your mind, attempting to reenter it as closely as possible.
4. Tell yourself you're going back to the dreamscape.
5. Expect to return to this dream as if this is something you regularly do. (Expectation has a strong influence on outcome.)
6. Imagine yourself standing and spinning, turning around and around as you reenter the dream.

If you have trouble getting back into the dream, pretend you have and use your imagination and fantasy to be wherever you want to be and finish the dream as you like.

APPENDIX N
Norms (General Directions) for Dream Groups

1. Do not interrupt the dreamer while he/she is telling the dream.
2. Confidentiality. Anything discussed during dream groups should be considered confidential information. Do not repeat dreams and the meaning for the dreamer with any information that would identify the dreamer.
3. Use "I" statements when talking about another's dream. "If it were my dream. . ."
4. Don't begin your sentences with "You." Phrase questions tentatively and avoid telling the dreamer what something means or how she/he REALLY feels. Do not tell the dreamer what you think the dream means for him/her.
5. Promptness. Be on time. This shows respect for other group members and allows all to have the session complete with touch-in, breathing, hearing entire dreams, closure.
6. **Do** use the group as an opportunity to ask for encouragement, feedback, validation, support. Let us know about your artwork, creative projects, and goals so we can cheer you on. Brag about your accomplishments.
7. Avoid giving advice, criticism, or making judgments about the decisions of others. YMMV (Your mileage may vary).
8. Try to relax your usual constraints on language, tears, political correctness.
9. Speak aloud the way you would speak to yourself, in your own terms. Dream groups go stale if people are trying to be polite and proper.

10. Focus on positives, strengths, improvement: How does the dream offer a more hopeful future?
11. Dream insights require action. What insights do you have at the end of the group and how will you take them into action in your own life?

APPENDIX O
Gestalt Empty Chair Technique

1. The dreamer chooses two chairs and arranges them so that the characters might have a dialogue. She might place the chairs facing each other or have them side by side. The dreamer, not the therapist or facilitator, should choose the arrangement.
2. The dreamer sits in one chair and opens the dialogue with the other character imagined in the empty chair. This could be anyone: a child, a parent or sibling, an ex-spouse or current lover. The person may be living or dead or an unknown figure, object, or animal from a dream or fantasy.
3. When the dreamer expects the other person to speak or asks a question of the other person, the dreamer then enters the empty chair and speaks for this person. It is helpful if the dreamer can play the part of this person as authentically as possible, using any speech pattern, gesture, or voice that the dreamer would recognize as characteristic of this person.
4. When that character has responded, the dreamer will switch to the first chair and speak again as herself.
5. This continues until there is some movement or shift in the conversation. Perhaps some feelings that were out of awareness are brought to the surface or a new way of seeing a conflict is revealed. This often helps the dreamer to gain a

perspective that was unavailable before the dialogue. The new perspective is the first step in taking action.

6. The dreamer will know when the dialogue has come to a natural close. Sometimes, if a lot of feelings have been generated, stopping the dialogue to process what has shifted or been revealed might be the best idea.

7. This technique works well in dream groups or with dream partners since having others present will help in seeing the many angles and perspectives that the dialogue revealed.

APPENDIX P
Suggestions for Dealing with Insomnia

1. Use your bed ONLY for sleep and sex. Read, ruminate, talk, or think in other places. Your bed should be a discriminative stimulus for sleep.

2. Never stay in bed and toss and turn. Get up if you don't feel sleepy, no matter what the hour. Go back to bed when you feel sleepy.

3. If you don't fall asleep within fifteen minutes of going to bed, get up and occupy yourself with some relaxing and enjoyable task such as reading or writing. Do this in another room. Watching television works for some, but it may also stimulate you.

4. Return to bed and repeat #2 and #3 until you feel sleepy again.

5. Use natural tranquilizers such as a glass of skim milk at bedtime, hot herbal tea without caffeine, a warm bath or shower, deep breathing and other progressive relaxation exercises.

6. Make love or masturbate at bedtime or if you wake up and are unable to fall back to sleep. An orgasm is the best seda-

tive for many people and is good for the health of your mind and body.

7. If you have thoughts crowding your mind and keeping you awake, write them down. Make lists of things to do or to remember so you don't worry about forgetting them. When you write things down, you can put them aside mentally.

8. Experiment. Do what works best for you. Notice when you get a good night's sleep and what the preceding day was like. Repeat what works.

9. Look into tapes or literature designed to encourage the relaxation response. The self-hypnosis tapes work very well for some, and they are inexpensive and safe.

10. Do not take sleeping pills or tranquilizers of any kind. They usually increase insomnia and anxiety and most are habit-forming. Tell your doctor you'd rather deal with your sleeplessness in a natural way. These medications also turn off your dreaming and REM sleep.

11. Make sure your day includes enough physical activity. Exercise, even just walking, improves sleep. Exercise near bedtime causes sleeplessness for some because it increases energy and awakens the mind. Learn how your body responds best.

12. Do not consume products with caffeine near bedtime. For some people, this means abstaining from these products as much as five hours before bedtime, depending on your sensitivity to caffeine. Remember: this includes coffee, chocolate, anything prepared with chocolate, tea, many soft drinks such as colas, and some over-the-counter medications. Read labels for contents.

13. Use prayer or meditation at bedtime if you find it relaxing. For some people, prayer is like saying a mantra. You might consider saying to yourself "sleepy, sleepy, sleepy." This is a form of self-hypnosis too.

14. Limit or eliminate your use of alcohol. Drinking alcohol,

even in small quantities, causes a rebound effect in some people, resulting in their waking during the night. Try giving up drinking alcohol entirely for two or more weeks and see whether you sleep any better.

15. Keep a dream diary and appreciate your dreams as a way to self-knowledge and peace. A dream is a window to your unconscious.

16. Talk about the issues that trouble you. If you feel you can't talk to your spouse/mate/lover about something for ANY reason, seek out another friend. Otherwise, consider getting professional or pastoral help.

17. Know that people are different and need different amounts of sleep. This will change at different times in your life. People usually sleep less as they grow older. Consider the possibility that the amount of sleep you are getting which seems little to you might be *enough for you.*

18. Recognize that chronic sleep problems can be symptomatic of a wide variety of psychological and physical changes or disturbances, including ordinary passages such as menopause. Asking for professional advice might be helpful.

19. Change your attitude about sleepless nights. Look at all the extra time you have when you're not sleeping as a gift to do things you never had time to do before.

20. Be patient while expecting a change in your sleep pattern.

APPENDIX Q
Relaxation Exercise

1. Choose a comfortable chair where you can sit with your back straight and your feet flat on the floor. Rest your hands comfortably in your lap. Don't clasp them. Find a position where they are at rest without any pressure.

2. If you are comfortable sitting on the floor or a cushion with your legs crossed and without a backrest, this is preferable for meditation, but not necessary. You may also lie down flat if you prefer, but many people fall asleep in this position. If you do fall asleep, consider the possibility that your body might be telling you that you need this deeper rest. Do this exercise while reclining if it is a preparation for going to sleep.

3. Once in a comfortable position, close your eyes. Take some long, deep breaths. Mentally count to six with each inhale and exhale. Bring your awareness to the rise and fall of your belly. If you find yourself breathing from your chest, breathe from your belly or abdomen instead. This is deeper and more healthful and restful.

4. Continue deep breathing and bring your awareness to your toes.

5. Relax your toes. Relax your feet. Let go of all the tension in your feet and ankles. See the tension draining out of you. Tighten and relax the muscles of your legs. Then relax your calves, your knees, your thighs. Feel your muscles releasing their tension and the tightness. They are warm and relaxed.

6. Relax your groin, your abdomen, your chest. Feel yourself letting go and becoming more and more relaxed. Relax your throat, shoulders, and upper arms. Relax your lower arms. Feel how limp and relaxed your hands and wrists are. Relax your back and your neck. All the tension has left your body.

7. Now relax your face. Open your mouth wide and then let it close comfortably. Moisten your lips. Relax your mouth and lips, your tongue. Relax your cheeks and nose. Relax your forehead and your scalp. They are soft and at ease.

8. Feel yourself floating or perhaps sinking into the chair or floor. You are warm, completely relaxed, calm, and cozy.

9. Stay perfectly still and enjoy this feeling. Know that it is always available to you.

10. At any time you are feeling tense or tight, spend a few minutes consciously relaxing your body. Even a few deep breaths in moments of crisis or pressure will help you relax and center yourself. You can use this to help you think more clearly and effectively.

APPENDIX R
Meditation Instruction

There are many different kinds of meditation for different purposes and many excellent books on this subject. Some of these are listed in the bibliography. (See Jack Kornfield, Joseph Goldstein, Ram Dass, Thich Nhat Hanh, Charles Tart.) For first-time mediators, I highly recommend Lawrence LeShan's *How to Meditate.*

People meditate for many reasons: to relax, to get in touch with their bodies and their emotions, to observe the flow of their thoughts, to quiet the mind, to contemplate a decision or a particular issue, to journey in their imaginations, to feel at-one-ment with the universe. All these have their benefits and specific outcomes. Each may be seen as its own spiritual path to enlightenment or growth.

If you would like to add a simple meditation in preparation for dreamwork, journal writing, or any other form of inner work, try using the meditation of the breath.

1. Begin with a relaxation exercise such as the preceding one in this Appendix.
2. Once fully relaxed, bring your mental focus back to your breath. With eyes closed, begin counting your respirations up to four. Each full cycle of exhale and inhale is one respiration. When you get to four, begin again at the number one.
3. Do this for fifteen minutes at a time, once a day to start.

Having regular time to do this each day is helpful for the discipline.

4. Your mind will wander. You will have a hard time staying focused on counting your breaths. Some minutes will probably pass and you will realize you have been lost in thoughts or a fantasy or planning what to eat for dinner. This is normal.
5. Gently bring your focus back to your breath. Do not scold yourself or think you're hopeless. This "monkey mind" is part of the human experience. That is one of the reasons why we meditate: to settle the mind.
6. Each time you find you've wandered from your focus, return to your breath. Feel your body. Be present to the sensation of breathing.

This is an excellent way to reduce stress and take a short break in a busy day. Even a few minutes can be very helpful. You do not need to take expensive classes in meditation or to have a guru. A teacher can be helpful and meditating with others often motivates new meditators to stay with the process longer than they would on their own, but it is not necessary. Choose your teachers and your meditation partners wisely since meditation puts you in a very suggestible state.

If you find that meditation makes you anxious or fearful, *STOP.* Write and/or talk about the feelings and thoughts that came up for you. Some people experience what is now called Relaxation Induced Anxiety. Their jittery, nervous feelings sometimes get worse with meditation or relaxation exercises. (See Singer, 1995.) Over time, this usually diminishes, but always address whatever feelings arise. Whatever you experience, it is normal for you. Talk to others about your experiences and you will discover how common these "weird" feelings are. Doing a short meditation before any creative work, before writing in your journal, or before dreamwork will be helpful.

APPENDIX S
Meditation of the White Light

This meditation is suitable for use at the end of dream groups, but it can be used at any time.

1. Stand in a circle. Position left palm up, right palm down and join hands.
2. Feel your feet planted firmly in the ground.
3. Let your body relax.
4. Be aware of the sensation of the hands in yours; be present to the person on either side of you.
5. Breathe deeply. Take a few deep breaths, aware of this circle of people who are your dream partners.
6. Imagine you are standing in a cone of white, healing light. See this cone of light shining over your head.
7. The cone of light expands, including the other members of the dream group, sending a healing, comforting, warm light.
8. As the cone expands, it moves out to include the building you are in, then out to the streets and the other buildings.
9. The cone of light expands, growing larger to include all the neighborhood, the city, the state.
10. The light continues to grow, bathing all the states, the country, and finally the world in this white light.
11. The light sends wisdom and healing to all the people, the world leaders, the men and women with power and decisions to make, healing them of their hurts.
12. Out into the universe, the cone fills all in its white light.
13. Pause for a minute and continue deep breathing.
14. Slowly, see the cone of light contracting, getting smaller to shine on just our planet Earth.
15. Then contracting again to shine on our country, then this state, this building, this dream group together.

16. See the cone of light over your head and then slowly open your eyes.
17. Until next time . . .

APPENDIX T
Dream Test

♦ Do you ever have dreams that leave you feeling confused or troubled?

♦ Do you dream about your work or future?

♦ Do you wonder what your dreams mean?

♦ Do you ever fear your dreams might come true?

♦ Do you have a recurrent nightmare?

♦ Do you have a recurrent dream theme or symbol?

♦ Would you like to know what your personal symbols mean?

♦ Do you dream about people who are no longer in your life?

♦ Do you have sexual dreams that embarrass or surprise you?

♦ Do you have dreams that leave you with fear or anxiety?

♦ Would you like to be able to dream about a specific topic?

♦ Do your dreams seem bizarre or weird to you?

♦ Would you like to use dreams for problem solving?

♦ Do you have vivid dreams that feel more real than life?

♦ Would you like to have lucid dreams?

♦ Would you like to be able to have more pleasant dreams?

♦ Would you like to use dream information for your personal growth?

♦ Do you dream of hurricanes, tornadoes, earthquakes, or other disasters?

♦ Do you have dreams of rape, attack, or of being chased?

♦ Would you like to use dream material to stimulate your creativity?

♦ Would you like to use dreams to improve your personal relationships?

♦ Would you like to use your dream wisdom to have more success?

♦ Do you wonder whether dreams are warnings about your health or safety?

If you've answered yes to any of these questions, you can benefit from doing dreamwork.

BIBLIOGRAPHY

Adams, Kathleen. 1990. *Journal to the Self: Twenty-two Paths to Personal Growth.* Warner Books.

Alvarez, A. 1995. *Night: Night Life, Night Language Sleep, and Dreams.* Norton.

Assagioli, Roberto. 1973. *The Act of Will.* Penguin.

———. 1965. *Psychosynthesis.* Viking.

Bass, Ellen, and Davis, L. 1988. *The Courage to Heal.* HarperPerennial.

Borcherdt, Bill. 1989. *Think Straight! Feel Great!* Professional Resource Exchange, Inc.

———. 1993. *You Can Control Your Feelings!* Professional Resource Press, Inc.

Cameron, Julia. 1992. *The Artist's Way.* Jeremy P. Tarcher/Perigee.

———. 1996. *The Vein of Gold.* Jeremy P. Tarcher/Putnam.

Capacchione, Lucia. 1979. *The Creative Journal.* Newcastle.

Conway, Flo, and Siegelman, Jim. 1978. *Snapping: America's Epidemic of Sudden Personality Change.* Stillpoint Press.

Cooper, D. Jason. 1995. *The Power of Dreaming.* Llewellyn Publications.

Delaney, Gayle. 1991. *Breakthrough Dreaming*. Bantam.

———. 1994. *Sexual Dreams*. Fawcett Columbine.

Dement, William C. 1972. *Some Must Watch While Some Must Sleep*. Norton.

Dodson, Betty. 1996. *Sex for One: The Joy of Selfloving*. Crown Trade Paperbacks.

Epel, Naomi (ed). 1993. *Writers Dreaming*. Carol Southern Books.

Faraday, Ann. 1974. *The Dream Game*. Perennial/ Harper & Row.

———. 1972. *Dream Power*. Berkley Medallion.

Feinstein, D., and Krippner, S. 1988. *Personal Mythology*. Jeremy P. Tarcher.

Ferber, Richard. 1985. *Solve Your Child's Sleep Problems*. Simon & Schuster.

Ferrucci, Piero. 1982. *What We May Be*. Jeremy P. Tarcher/Putnam.

Fincher, Suzanne F. 1991. *Creating Mandalas*. Shambhala.

Forward, Susan. 1989. *Toxic Parents*. Bantam.

Fritz, Roger. 1993. *Sleep Disorders*. National Sleep Alert, Inc.

Gackenbach, J., and LaBerge, S. (eds). 1988. *Conscious Mind, Sleeping Brain*. Plenum Press.

Gackenback, Jayne (ed). 1991. *Dream Images: A Call to Mental Arms*. Baywood Publishing.

Gallegos, E.S. 1985. *The Personal Totem Pole*. Moon Bear Press.

Garfield, Patricia. 1974. *Creative Dreaming*. Ballantine.

Goldberg, Natalie. 1990. *Wild Mind*. Bantam Books.

———. 1986. *Writing Down the Bones*. Shambhala.

Goldhammer, John D. 1996. *Under the Influence: The Destructive Effects of Group Dynamics*. Prometheus Books.

Goldstein, Joseph. 1976. *The Experience of Insight*. Shambhala.

Goldstein, J., and Kornfield, J. 1987. *Seeking the Heart of Wisdom*. Shambhala.

Gottman, John. 1994. *Why Marriages Succeed or Fail*. Simon & Schuster.

Grof, Stanislav, and Grof, C. (eds). 1989. *Spiritual Emergency*. Jeremy P. Tarcher/Perigee.

Hall, Calvin S. 1966. *The Meaning of Dreams*. McGraw-Hill.

Hall, James. 1983. *Jungian Dream Interpretation*. Inner City Books.

Hanh, Thich Nhat. 1993. *The Blooming of a Lotus*. Beacon Press.

———. 1975. *The Miracle of Mindfulness*. Beacon Press.

Harary, K., and Weintraub, P. 1989. *Lucid Dreams in 30 Days*. St. Martin's.

Harman, W., and Rheingold, H. 1984. *Higher Creativity*. Jeremy P. Tarcher, Inc.

Harner, Michael. 1980. *The Way of the Shaman*. Harper SanFrancisco.

Harrington-Mackin, Deborah. 1994. *The Team Building Tool Kit*. New Directions Management Services, Inc.

Hawk, Medicine, and Grey Cat. 1990. *American Indian Ceremonies*. Inner Light Publications.

Hendricks, Gay. 1995. *Conscious Breathing*. Bantam Books.

Hillman, James. 1996. *The Soul's Code*. Random House.

Hillman, James, and Ventura, M. 1992. *We've Had a Hundred Years of Psychotherapy and the World's Getting Worse*. Harper SanFrancisco.

Hoyt, Michael F. 1995. *Brief Therapy and Managed Care*. Jossey-Bass.

Johnson, Robert A. 1986. *Inner Work*. Harper SanFrancisco.

———. 1991. *Owning Your Own Shadow: Understanding the Dark Side of the Psyche;* Harper SanFrancisco.

Jung, Carl G. 1974. *Dreams*. Princeton University Press.

———. 1964. *Man and His Symbols*. Dell.

———. 1989. *Memories, Dreams, and Reflections*. Vintage.

Kalweit, Holger. 1988. *Dreamtime and Inner Space: The World of the Shaman*. Shambhala.

Keyes, Daniel. 1981. *The Minds of Billy Milligan*. Bantam Books.

Keyes, Laurel Elizabeth. 1973. *Toning*. DeVORSS.

King, Stephen. 1981. *Danse Macabre*. Berkley.

Kornfield, Jack. 1993. *A Path with Heart*. Bantam.

Krakow, Barry, and Neidhardt, J. 1992. *Conquering Bad Dreams and Nightmares*. Berkley.

Krippner, Stanley. 1990. *Dreamtime and Dreamwork*. Jeremy P. Tarcher, Inc.

Kryger, Meir H. (ed). 1994. *Principles and Practice of Sleep Medicine*. W. B. Saunders Company.

Kurtz, Paul. 1991. *The Transcendental Temptation*. Prometheus.

LaBerge, Stephen. 1985. *Lucid Dreaming*. Ballantine.

LaBerge, S., and Rheingold, H. 1990. *Exploring the World of Lucid Dreaming*. Ballantine.

LeShan, Lawrence. 1974. *How to Meditate*. Bantam.

Loftus, E., and Ketchum, K. 1994. *The Myth of Repressed Memory*. St. Martin's Griffin.

————. 1991. *Witness for the Defense*. St. Martin's Press.

Louden, Jennifer. 1992. *The Woman's Comfort Book*. Harper San-Francisco.

Mariechild, Diane. 1981. *Mother Wit*. Crossing Press.

Masson, Jeffrey Moussaieff. 1988. *Against Therapy*. Common Courage Press.

Masters, Robert, and Houston, Jean. 1972. *Mind Games: The Guide to Inner Space*. Barnes & Noble.

Mindell, Arnold. 1982. *Dreambody*. Sigo Press.

Morris, Jill. 1985. *The Dream Workbook*. Fawcett Crest.

Moss, Robert. 1996. *Conscious Dreaming*. Crown.

Ofshe, Richard, and Watters, E. 1994. *Making Monsters*. Charles Scribner's Sons.

Ornstein, Robert, and Sobel, D. 1989. *Healthy Pleasures*. Addison-Wesley.

Perkins, John. 1990. *Psychonavigation*. Destiny Books.

————. 1994. *The World Is As You Dream It*. Destiny Books.

Perls, Frederick S. 1969. *Gestalt Therapy Verbatim*. Bantam.

Progoff, Ira. 1975. *At a Journal Workshop*. Jeremy P. Tarcher/Perigee.

Rainer, Tristine. 1978. *The New Diary*. Jeremy P. Tarcher, Inc.

Robbins, Anthony. 1986. *Unlimited Power*. Fawcett Columbine.

Roth, Gabrielle, and Loudon, J. 1989. *Maps to Ecstasy*. Nataraj Publishing.

Sher, Barbara. 1979. *Wishcraft*. Ballantine Books.

Shuman, Sandra. 1989. *Source Imagery*. Doubleday.

Signell, Karen. 1990. *Wisdom of the Heart*. Bantam.

Singer, Margaret, and Lalich, J. 1995. *Cults in Our Midst*. Jossey-Bass Publishers.

Starhawk. 1979. *The Spiral Dance*. Harper SanFrancisco.

———. 1987. *Truth or Dare*. Harper SanFrancisco.

Stevens, Jose, and Stevens, L. S. 1988. *The Secrets of Shamanism*. Avon.

Szasz, Thomas. 1961. *The Myth of Mental Illness*. Dell.

Tart, Charles 1994. *Living the Mindful Life*. Shambhala.

———. 1987. *Waking Up*. Shambhala.

Tart, Charles (ed). 1969. *Altered States of Consciousness*. Doubleday Anchor.

Taylor, Jeremy. 1983. *Dreamwork*. Paulist Press.

———. 1992. *Where People Fly and Water Runs Uphill*. Warner Books.

Terr, Lenore. 1994. *Unchained Memories*. Basic Books.

Ullman, Montague, and Zimmerman, N. 1979. *Working with Dreams*. Jeremy P. Tarcher/Perigee.

Van de Castle, Robert. 1994. *Our Dreaming Mind*. Ballantine.

Walsh, Roger. 1990. *The Spirit of Shamanism*. Jeremy P. Tarcher/Perigee.

Welwood, John (ed). 1992. *Ordinary Magic*. Shambhala.

White, J., and Fadiman, J. (eds). 1976. *Relax*. The Confucian Press.

Whitmont, Edward, and Perera, S. 1989. *Dreams, A Portal to the Source*. Routledge.

Williamson, Gay and David. 1994. *Transformative Rituals*. Health Communications, Inc.

Wolinsky, Stephen. 1991. *Trances People Live*. Bramble Company.

Yalom, Irvin. 1975. *The Theory and Practice of Group Psychotherapy*. Basic Books.

Yapko, Michael. 1994. *Suggestions of Abuse*. Simon & Schuster.

Zweig, Connie, and Abrams, J. 1991. *Meeting the Shadow*. Jeremy P. Tarcher/Putnam.

INDEX

ABOUT THE AUTHOR

Photo by Richard Nathanson

Joan Mazza is the author of *Dreaming Your Real Self: A Personal Approach to Dream Interpretation* (Perigee/Putnam, July 1998), and the forthcoming *Dream Back Your Life: Taking Your Dream Messages into Life Action*. She is a psychotherapist and licensed mental health counselor. She holds a master's degree in counseling psychology and conducts ongoing groups in South Florida as well as national seminars. She teaches a variety of other topics including:

- How to Say No With a Smile: Setting Personal Boundaries
- Managing Your Emotions
- When Life Gives You Lemons . . .
- Conscious Sexuality

As a speaker, Joan Mazza brings seminars to both professionals and the public, addressing the concerns and frustrations of people in "mid-life" crises regardless of age. With humor and personal anecdotes, she invites people to be themselves, take risks, and dream back their lives.

She is a past-president of The Book Group of South Florida, an organization of authors and book industry professionals. Her short stories, articles, poetry, and essays have appeared in many publications.

She lives in Fort Lauderdale, Florida, with her two poodles, Bambi and Razz-ma-Tazz.

Joan Mazza, M.S., is available as a speaker or seminar leader for your corporation or organization. Audiotapes and other instructional materials are also available. For more information

Call toll-free (888) DREAM-30
www. joanmazza.com

OTHER BOOKS OF INTEREST